Making Original Dolls of Composition, Bisque, and Porcelain

Other Books by the Author

THE ART of MAKING CLOTH TOYS
THE ART of PUPPETS and MARIONETTES
DRESSING DOLLS
MAKING DOLLHOUSE ACCESSORIES
TOYS: A STEP-BY-STEP GUIDE to CREATIVE TOYMAKING

Making Original Dolls of Composition, Bisque, and Porcelain

by
Charlene Davis Roth
Photography by James A. Davis

CROWN PUBLISHERS, INC. NEW YORK

441 3837

To my daughter, Amy

3.17.81 Baker 761

Library of Congress Cataloging in Publication Data
Roth, Charlene Davis, 1945–
  Making original dolls of composition, bisque, and porcelain.

  Bibliography: p.
  Includes index.
  1. Dollmaking. I. Title.
TT175.R67 1980   745.59'22   79-17413
        ISBN: 0-517-537176

Design by Leonard Henderson
10 9 8 7 6 5 4 3 2 1 First edition

CONTENTS

INTRODUCTION

The text of *Making Original Dolls of Composition, Bisque, and Porcelain* is an exploration of the ancient, time-honored craft of dollmaking, updated with modern methods and materials, stressing originality and, it is to be hoped, mapping out the route for the dollmaker to take a giant step into the world of art. But, more specifically, here are carefully explained the procedures and techniques used to produce dolls in each of the three plastic mediums—composition, bisque, and porcelain. The explanations are augmented by illustrations, and, wherever possible, specific patterns are included. For the dollmaker who wishes to do so, recipes are given for making a variety of necessary supplies ranging from composition to a china-painting medium. Information is included for making simple composition dolls from ingredients purchased at the local grocery store and requiring no more equipment than is contained in an ordinary kitchen. Yet, also included are complete instructions for the more complicated techniques of clay modeling, making plaster molds, pouring porcelain slip, and china painting the high-fired doll. Ten step-by-step projects for enthusiasts who wish to practice before designing their own dolls can be found within. The projects describe in text, diagrams, and patterns the procedures for making complete dolls in each of the three mediums, and for making their clothing, too. In short, *Making Original Dolls of Composition, Bisque, and Porcelain* contains all the information to encourage the beginner to make a first doll and the intermediate to make a first original doll as well as information that may help the advanced dollmaker become more proficient within the craft of dollmaking.

1–1 Pen-and-ink sketch of ancient Greek
terra-cotta toy doll.

CHAPTER 1
A Brief History of Dollmaking

It would be easy to assume that dolls have existed as playthings since early man first had time to take his mind off the business of survival and to fashion one. But this does not appear to be the case. Nature was probably the first dollmaker. The wind or the ocean shaped a log or rock into a human form, and primitive people stumbled across her invention. They were most likely filled with awe. Primitive people had little understanding of natural phenomena. They imagined that obscure mystical forces controlled their existence and most likely they would have imagined that these same forces invested the figure.

Man matured, and he began to share the role of dollmaker with Mother Nature. At first, he used natural forms that suggested the human figure and added bits of carving and color to enhance the likeness. Eventually, the doll figures were entirely of his own design. Still, they were not toys. Scholars have established that the earliest existing dolls are ancestor images. The dolls were created to represent a relative who had died. It was believed the doll would assimilate the spirit of the dead and prevent its doing harm to the living.

Dollmakers began to produce tiny doll images at about this same time. These have been labeled fetishes, amulets, and talismans. The dolls were thought to be capable of protecting, healing, or revenging the person who carried one.

The votive image and funeral image made their appearance next. These dolls required more skill of the dollmaker. They were created in the likeness of a living person and took his/her place during certain religious ceremonies.

It is safe to assume that prehistoric dollmakers reserved their creations for mystical and religious duties. It is equally safe to assume (because of the evidence of excavations) that, with the appearance of civilized cultures, there also appeared toy dolls. At what point in between dollmakers began to fashion dolls as playthings is not known. It has been suggested by knowledgeable sources that, with the passage of time, some of the images lost their religious or supernatural significance. They were no longer useful to the adults. So, though they were not produced to be toys, they were turned over to the children and became toys. The transition was probably gradual with similar dolls serving dual purposes for a period of time.

The earliest examples of toy dolls uncovered by archaeologists belonged to the ancient Egyptians. The dollmakers used clay, wood, or linen stuffed with papyrus strips for the forms of these early toy dolls. Features and hair were often embroidered. Some of the dolls had movable limbs as well as fabric gar-

1

ments and jewelry. An example of an Egyptian toy doll dating from the year 1900 B.C. is on display in a German museum.

Other ancient civilizations, namely, the Greeks and Romans, have left firm evidence that the toy doll was a common item. Literary references occur and dolls have been discovered in the graves of children of the time. A well-documented event, practiced by both cultures, was the dedication of a young girl's dolls to a goddess at the time of her betrothal.

The toy doll gained in popularity during the Middle Ages. A European literary work of the eighth or ninth century mentions rag dolls, but the earliest tangible examples are of baked clay and were made during the thirteenth or fourteenth century. A fledgling doll industry was probably in existence at this time, because a number of replicas of the same figure were uncovered during excavations at the city of Tannenberg, Germany. European literature, illustrations, and paintings mention or portray toy dolls at increasingly frequent intervals from the fifteenth century onward.

Wood has been a primary source of material for dolls from their introduction until the nineteenth century, when other materials gained in popularity. During the Middle Ages, wood was less expensive and more available to the dollmaker than was fabric or clay. Germany, which was blessed with large untapped forests, became an early leader in the production of dolls. The first German dolls were called *Tocke*, originally defined as a block of wood, which apparently is what the dolls resembled—little more than a block of wood.

By the early sixteenth century, the status of toy dolls had begun to improve. Records state that beautifully dressed dolls were being offered for sale along with other luxuries. These highly priced dolls were purchased by the aristocracy. However, the average dollmaker continued to produce inexpensive wooden dolls for general consumption.

Concurrent with the production of toy dolls throughout this era, dollmakers were busy making dolls for another purpose. These dolls, called fashion dolls, were dressed in the latest fashions and sent to a dressmaker's clientele. They were the fashion designers' first reliable method of advertising their products over long distances. The dolls appeared long before technical processes for printing illustrations had been developed, and remained in favor even after these processes were perfected. Dolls were used for advertising clothes and hairdos until the fashion magazine took precedence in the late nineteenth century.

The eighteenth century foreshadowed, but the nineteenth century brought great change to the world of dollmaking. New methods, new materials, and the emergence of several outstanding artists in the field changed the doll immeasurably.

Wax, as a medium for dolls, was in use for centuries, but the early wax dolls could not compete with the quality of those constructed of wood. By the nineteenth century, however, dollmakers began to experiment with wax. They perfected a variety of techniques. The wax was molded, modeled, or applied in a layer over another material such as wood or composition. Beautiful, lifelike wax dolls, with glowing skin and ample and curvaceous form, began to be produced.

Another material gaining wide usage among dollmakers during the nineteenth century was composition (which also includes papier-mâché). An early reference claims papier-mâché (literally, chewed paper) was in use for making dolls in France as long ago as 1540. It did not, however, gain wide popularity until the first decade of the nineteenth century, when the Germans developed a method of pressure-molding papier-mâché and began to mass-produce these dolls. This material and the process involved are said to have been responsible for establishing the colossal German doll industry of the nineteenth and early twentieth centuries.

Bisque (unglazed ceramics), as a material from which to make dolls, also came into its own during the nineteenth century. It has been used prior to this time, as had many of the other materials, but it was not fully appreciated until the mid-1800s. Bisque dolls were made famous by the artistry of two French dollmakers, Jumeau and Bru. Their dolls are a favorite of collectors today. Their beauty and craftsmanship are exceptional.

China (glazed ceramic) dolls also became very popular during the nineteenth century. They were the product of factories. Made primarily of porcelain, the dolls required firing at high temperatures. This was impractical for small-scale dollmakers before the introduction of the electric kiln. Germany was the leader in the production of the china dolls.

The twentieth century has brought more change to the world of the doll. Durable rubber, cellulose, and plastic dolls poured and still pour by the millions from factories. In volume and longevity, they eclipse the fragile dolls of the previous century. The individual dollmaker or small dollmaking family has become a rarity. The majority of dolls are now products of large corporations.

CHAPTER 2
A Guide to Terms and Symbols

The text of *Making Original Dolls of Composition, Bisque, and Procelain* has been arranged in a straightforward manner to make it an uncomplicated, effective tool for the use of the reader/craftsperson. Here is a brief description of the design that is followed throughout: First, the book has been divided into three general sections, namely, composition, bisque, and porcelain. The sections are arranged to proceed from the least complicated to the more specialized medium. Composition appears first because it requires no uncommon equipment and the techniques can be easily mastered. Bisque demands a little more skill on the part of the dollmaker and the work must be fired (necessitating renting firing time or a home kiln), so it has been allocated second place. Porcelain dollmaking, which involves the more finicky procedures of high-firing and china painting, is reserved for the last section. Each section begins with an in-depth discussion of the properties of the material to be explored. Procedures and techniques, developing a work area, necessary and helpful tools, and sources of supply are covered. Occasionally, more than one successful route to the same end is described, leaving the choice of direction up to the individual dollmaker. After each discussion of medium follows a series of dollmaking projects that put the medium to use. These also proceed from simple to more complicated procedures. I advise reading the information contained within the projects even if the reader plans to make only original dolls. Here is where you will find information on wigmaking, designing cloth bodies, and assembling and dressing dolls. Each doll project is unique and explores a different aspect of the dollmaking technique. Materials or projects that overlap will be cross-referenced, to avoid repetition.

Every craft has a language of its own and the craft of dollmaking is no exception. Terms denoting tools, materials, and procedures occur throughout the following chapters. Many of these terms may not have been encountered by the reader. To facilitate communication, a list of words related to the craft of dollmaking, and their definitions, appears after the main body of the text. You may wish to establish a passing familiarity with any new words by reading through the list. This glossary can also be used as a reference, to clarify a point, when the reader is at work on an original doll or one of the projects.

Just as every craft has a language of its own, so does every craft book. A number of signs and symbols are marked on the patterns that appear in the following pages. They are guides to cutting and stitching. An illustration and an explanation of each mark follow.

4

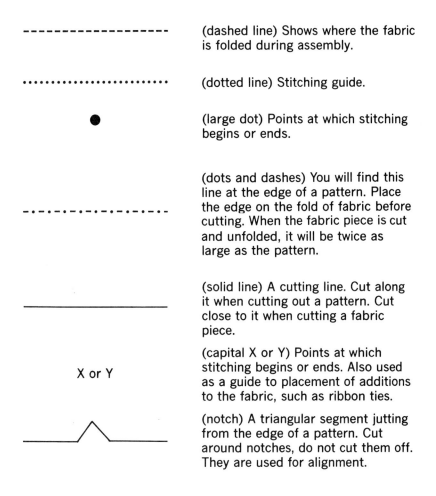

------------------- (dashed line) Shows where the fabric is folded during assembly.

.... (dotted line) Stitching guide.

● (large dot) Points at which stitching begins or ends.

-.-.-.-.-.-.-.- (dots and dashes) You will find this line at the edge of a pattern. Place the edge on the fold of fabric before cutting. When the fabric piece is cut and unfolded, it will be twice as large as the pattern.

_____ (solid line) A cutting line. Cut along it when cutting out a pattern. Cut close to it when cutting a fabric piece.

X or Y (capital X or Y) Points at which stitching begins or ends. Also used as a guide to placement of additions to the fabric, such as ribbon ties.

(notch) A triangular segment jutting from the edge of a pattern. Cut around notches, do not cut them off. They are used for alignment.

IDENTIFYING MARKS AND COPYRIGHTS

If you take the time and expend the energy to produce an original doll of which you are proud, you will want the public to be aware that you produced it. For this purpose, dolls, like paintings, are signed. A signature on a doll is called a mark. You can use your name or initials or even devise a symbol. But keep your mark consistent. If you produce a body of work you will want it all recognized as your own. Also, it is standard practice to follow the mark with the date on which the doll was designed.

Marks are found almost everywhere on dolls. They appear on the soles of the feet, inside the head, and even on the eyeball. The most popular place is the back of the head or the back of the shoulder. If you use a store-bought composition body and add an original head, be sure to sign the head.

Clay dolls can be permanently marked by incising the surface of the damp model. If the doll is made of composition, paint your mark with acrylic paint and varnish the dry signature with acrylic varnish.

A serious dollmaker, producing unique and innovative work, should consider copywriting his/her creations. Booklets explaining copyright law can be obtained from the federal government. Write to Copyright Office, Library of Congress, Washington, D.C. 20540. Also, ask for "G" blanks to be sent with your order. These are the correct forms to file when copyrighting a doll.

If you make a doll that you are planning to copyright, incise the back of the neck with ©, your full name, the year, and the doll's name. The Copright Office will require two representative heads or two sets of photographs clearly showing the detail of the doll, including the identifying marks. Mail these, plus a filled-out form "G" and six dollars (check or money order), to the Copyright Office. It will take an average of three and one-half months for the information to be processed and the copyright established. Once a copyright is obtained, it is good for the length of the copyrighter's life plus an additional fifty years.

CHAPTER 3
Designing a doll

Designing an original doll is a creative process. It is a spiritual and technical combination. The dollmaker must have a vision of a doll, but also the skill to turn the vision into tangible form. Dolls are sculptures. They are three-dimensional figures modeled, molded, or carved from plastic materials. They are not just accurate reproductions of the human form. To be successful, a doll, like a sculpture, should reflect the personality of the dollmaker.

To begin, develop a concept. Picture in your mind the doll you hope to create. The first mental image of the doll and the actual creation will most likely be worlds apart, but you must begin somewhere. Do not be afraid to change the original concept as you progress. This is how character is developed.

Research the image you have created. If, for example, the doll is to be a character from literature, reread the story. If you have envisioned her in the style of an antique doll, study photographs of the period, or visit museum and private doll collections. For the sake of this and future dolls, start a scrapbook or a file containing clippings of photographs and drawings that portray interesting hairdos, unusual features, a close-up of an ear or an eye. Full figures at rest or in action make good reference material. As an art student, I collected newspaper photographs from the sports pages featuring such things as basketball players springing for the ball. Leafing through such a collection will sometimes make clear a hazy point of your design. Use the information you gather to bring the image of the doll into sharp focus. When you can visualize it from every angle, describe the hairdo, and form clear mental images of the clothing, you are ready for the next step, transferring the idea into tangible form.

A dollmaker should be able to sketch—either to draw on paper or to do quick three-dimensional renderings in clay. The doll design that can not be transferred to paper or clay is stillborn. But don't panic. Drawing and modeling are skills that can be learned. They are not mystical powers with which a few are blessed; both are based on observation. The serious dollmaker sees more than a swiftly moving scene. Learn to study people with whom you come in contact. Observe structure and proportion. Note facial expressions as well as postures. Pay attention to the appearance of the human form and the positions it assumes. Develop your powers of perception to a high point and then educate your hand to reproduce what the eyes now clearly see.

I think the best advice I can give is practice, practice, and more practice. Practice observing and practice making your observations tangible. This is an ongoing process. Don't wait until you can draw and model like Michelangelo

3–1   Preliminary sketches for "The Goose Girl"
(Project Six).

before beginning to work on your first doll. But, do begin developing these skills when you begin dollmaking. As you become more proficient, your dolls will improve. Observing, drawing, and modeling the human figure are skills that the dollmaker will want to keep honed to perfection throughout her career.

Eventually, to better reproduce the surface of the human form, you may wish to know how the skeletal and muscular systems of the body affect the shape of the surface. There are helpful books, presenting anatomy for the artist, available at most book and art supply stores. A few such books are listed at the back of this text in a section entitled "Books and Other Publications of Interest to the Dollmaker."

If you have a clear mental image of the doll you wish to design, the next step is to do a series of quick line drawings or a rough clay rendering of your subject. The beginner may be more comfortable with clay. It is easier to model a form than to draw its facsimile on paper, because of the problem of foreshortening. Do try a few quick sketches to fix your idea on paper and continue perfecting your drawing skills by practicing sketching between dolls. When you have made a clay model or a line drawing that successfully captures your concept of the doll, find a place to display it near where you will be making the doll. You will find yourself referring to these preliminary perceptions often.

The following pages explore three plastic mediums and all related techniques and procedures necessary to turn your drawings or clay model into an original doll.

CHAPTER 4
A Word about Fabric and Sewing Procedures for the Dollmaker

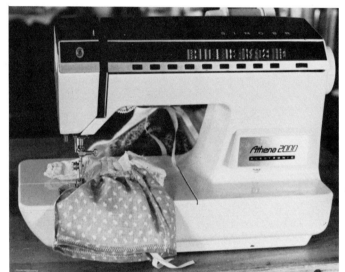

4–1   Sewing machine.

An attractive outfit can make an everyday doll something special, whereas a poorly constructed costume will detract from the beauty of a pretty doll. Some dollmakers never become involved in this aspect of the craft. They hire others to dress their dolls or purchase ready-made doll clothing. For those of you who are interested in dressing your own dolls or plan to tackle one of the following projects, here are some suggestions.

FABRICS

Use good quality fabrics. If you take the time to make an outfit for a doll, you want it to last. Quality fabrics are not necessarily heavy-weight fabrics. Delicate fabrics should also be well made. Check labels on bolts of fabric to see if the materials are colorfast and washable. Though these properties are not strictly necessary, they often indicate a good grade of fabric. A thread count is also an indication of fabric quality. The more threads to the square inch, the stronger the weave. Cottons and cotton blends are easy to work with and make a good choice for doll clothing. To achieve special effects it is often necessary to use novelty fabrics such as fake fur. These fabrics are also available in a variety of grades. Compare fabrics before you choose.

For the projects that follow, I have suggested types of fabric and color patterns for you to use. Other fabrics and designs are equally suitable. The choice is yours. However, if I specify stretch fabrics (such as knit), do not substitute a fabric that does not stretch. Certain garments require stretch for an accurate fit. Also, when I call for a *yard* of fabric, I mean the piece must be 36 inches long and at least 36 inches wide.

Another point to keep in mind when choosing fabrics is that dolls are small. Choose small prints and patterns that won't overwhelm the doll.

The yardage necessary for making doll clothing is not large. You can use leftover scraps of fabric from other sewing projects. You can also salvage fabrics from outgrown or out-of-style clothing. The parts of the doll's clothes are small enough to be cut from portions of the discarded clothing that are not shabby. Another source of fabrics is the remnant counter. Here you can often find small pieces of unusual and expensive fabrics drastically reduced.

PATTERNS

If you plan to design the clothing for your dolls, your most important tools will be a pencil, a straightedge, and a tape measure. The key to patternmaking is measuring. Measure the doll and transcribe these measurements to lines on paper. Add ¼ inch for seams and ½ inch for hems. For example, measure an arm from shoulder to wrist, add ¼ inch for the seam and ½ inch for the hem. This measurement is the length of each side of a pattern for a set-in sleeve. Measure the circumference of the arm at its widest point. Add to this measurement for the seam and a little more for ease of fit. This is the width of your sleeve pattern, the line that connects the two sides. A template featuring small ellipses will aid drawing an accurate armhole curve. Put it all together and you have a basic sleeve pattern. Measuring assures fit and allows you to arrive at an elemental pattern; additions of style are up to the individual designer. Glance at the doll clothing presented in the projects to get an idea of a variety of pattern shapes and types of pattern pieces that unite to make certain garments.

If you are using a pattern from the book, place tracing paper over the pattern and copy it. Be sure to trace all the pattern markings (dots, dashes, solid lines, Xs, etc.). These markings are explained in Chapter Two. Also transfer to the paper the name of the piece and the number of pieces to be cut. Dimensions instead of patterns are given for the parts of the doll clothing that are rectangular. Make a pattern by using the measurements and drawing the rectangle on a sheet of paper. Cut out the rectangle. Pin it to the fabric.

PREPARING THE FABRIC

Always press the fabric before you pin on the patterns. Unpressed fabrics do not cut accurately. One wrinkle will change the fit of a small garment. After ironing, pin the pattern to the fabric. If the pattern shows a line of alternating dots and dashes, fold the fabric and pin this line along the fold. Remember to pin patterns to napped fabrics so the nap will run in the same direction on all garment pieces. Fabrics with one-way designs also require special placement of pattern pieces.

CUTTING

Sharp scissors are a necessity for accurately cutting the small pieces of doll clothing. You can get along with standard 7-inch dressmaker's scissors, but 5-inch blades make the cutting easier and more efficient. Cut along solid lines. Cut around; do not cut off notches. Notches are triangular shapes that protrude from the edge of the pattern. Do not remove patterns from the fabrics until you have transferred the markings from the patterns to the fabrics.

TRANSFERRING MARKINGS

To transfer the markings to the fabric you will need dressmaker's tracing paper (purchased at notion counters and fabric stores). A tracing wheel is also helpful, or you can use a blunt instrument that will not pierce the pattern.

Pattern markings (described and defined in Chapter Two) need to be transferred to the fabric because they are stitching guides. Refer to figure 4-2. Sandwich a sheet of tracing paper between the fabric and the pattern. The colored side of the tracing paper should be against the fabric. Pin the pattern, tracing paper, and fabric together. Trace over the markings on the pattern. Use just enough pressure to get a recognizable mark on the fabric. When tracing is finished, remove the pins and pattern and check to be sure all the markings were transferred accurately.

SEWING

You can sew doll clothing by hand or with a sewing machine. Sewing by machine is faster and, unless you are a patient and accomplished seamstress, sturdier. Any sewing machine that sews a tight, straight stitch will do. A machine that also stitches zigzags and other fancy stitches is helpful for finishing seams and adding decorative touches. Check your machine manual for proper settings for different fabrics.

One-quarter inch of fabric is allowed for the seams of the garments in this book and is a good width for the seams of doll clothing in general. Half an inch of fabric has been allotted for hems. Hems on doll's clothing are so tiny it is recommended they be stitched by hand or with a narrow, closely spaced machine zigzag stitch.

Unless it is otherwise stated, always stitch fabric pieces to one another with *right* sides together.

Try to choose threads that match the fabrics to give a professional appearance to your stitchery. Clear nylon thread is useful when hand-stitching the parts of fabric doll bodies together. It is strong and flexible. Another good choice, for machine-stitching, is cotton-wrapped polyester thread. The colors are true and the thread is sturdy.

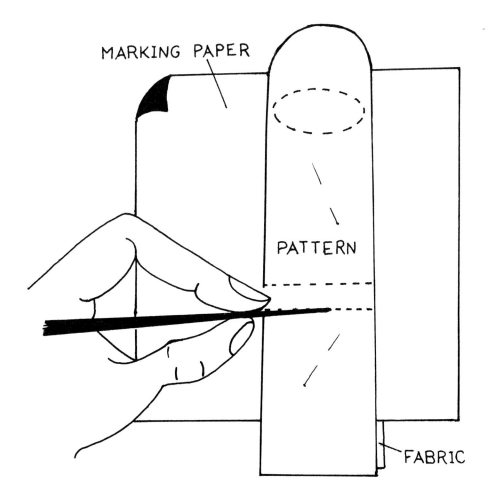

MARKING PAPER

PATTERN

FABRIC

4–2   Transferring markings from a pattern to the fabric.

FINISHING

Small snap closures, tiny buttons, ties, or hooks and eyes can be used to fasten a doll's clothing. Stitch these items securely to the fabric of the garments.

Lastly, trims are a dollmaker's treasure trove. They can spruce up and add a touch of uniqueness to any outfit. Trims are found in great variety and used in numerous ways. Lace, ruffles, beads, sequins, embroidery, ribbons, rhinestones, feathers, or rickrack can add vitality to the most humdrum ensemble.

Dressing dolls is one more way a dollmaker can display her creativity.

SECTION I

CHAPTER 5
Composition

Composition came into widespread use, as a material for dollmaking, during the 1800s. Often it was used as the ground beneath a layer of wax, but it also had a life of its own. The papier-mâché doll heads of Ludwig Grenier (possessor of the first U.S. patent for a doll head) are a good example of the doll artistry to be achieved with this material. Their broad faces, simple features, and dark hair have become classic examples of the composition doll.

Composition is an exciting, versatile medium. When wet, it is like clay. It can be pressed into molds or modeled over an armature. When dry, it has many of the properties of wood. It can be rasped, sanded, and carved. Unlike clay, it does not require firing or baking. Acrylic gesso, paints, and varnish provide an excellent durable finish for the surface.

Composition is a good material for the beginning dollmaker. It provides the novice with a chance to "try the craft on for size" while investing little in supplies. The main ingredients included in the composition recipes that follow are free or relatively inexpensive. Furthermore, the entire doll can be made at the kitchen table. A kitchen blender is the only recommended piece of equipment other than the kitchen stove. If you have a strong arm and a wire whisk, even the blender can be dispensed with.

On the other hand, it should be noted that the finished surface of the composition doll (as it is presented here) does not have the satin-smooth luster that bisque or porcelain enjoys. However, if time is spent rasping and sanding the dry surface, a close approximation can be obtained. I find there is an appealing, robust, folksy aura about the composition doll that makes it perfect for certain doll characters. And, a composition doll (made following the recipes and instructions presented here) can survive being dropped on a cement floor, a treatment I would never recommend for bisque or porcelain.

COMPOSITION RECIPES: I, II, and III

Over the centuries, composition recipes have included many different and unusual ingredients. Each manufacturer of composition dolls had a version, often "secret," of the composition recipe. These recipes contained common ingredients such as glue, sawdust, or shredded paper, but also less common ingredients like bread dough, cardboard, and old gloves. At one time, dollmakers were even known to taste their recipes (those containing flour) to determine if they had arrived at the correct proportion of ingredients.

16

Three recipes for composition follow. The primary ingredient of I and II is paper that has been reduced to pulp by means of cooking and beating. The first recipe is a hardy mixture of glossy magazine paper, kraft paper (brown grocery bags), glue, and other additives. The result is a light gray modeling compound, coarse grained and extremely tough when dry. This mixture was used for the head of Rumpelstiltskin (Project One) and the head and limbs of the Snow Queen (Project Two). The composition was applied over an armature. Recipe II, the basis of which is toilet paper, produces a white, fine-grained modeling material. This mixture was used to produce the dolls Hansel and Gretel (Project Three). The heads, torsos, and limbs of these dolls are hollow composition, formed in sized plaster molds. I found that the finer texture of Recipe II composition provided more accurate reproduction of the detail of the molds. Recipe III is a bread-dough composition. It is quick and easy to make. It can be stored in the refrigerator. It is useful for patching or applying last-minute detail.

Recipe I

Recipe I produces enough composition to make two doll heads, each having a circumference of 12 inches, and their arms and legs. The composition is applied over an armature. The pieces are not solid composition.

Materials

6 ounces of good quality paper such as glossy
    magazine paper
1 square foot of brown grocery-bag paper
2 tablespoons of whiting
4 tablespoons of white glue
1 tablespoon of linseed oil
2 tablespoons of dry powdered wheat wallpaper
    paste or ¼ cup flour and water paste
2 drops of oil of cloves or 1 tablespoon of Clorox

If you do not have a household or a postal scale, one half of an average *Newsweek* magazine is equivalent to 6 ounces. Whiting can be purchased at most large art-supply stores and hardware stores. Elmer's glue is an example of a suitable white glue. Either raw or boiled linseed oil can be used, but the boiled form dries more quickly, whereas the raw oil maintains optimum whiteness. If the doll you are making is intended for a young child who may chew on your creation, *do not* use wheat wallpaper paste—it is vermin-proofed. Mix up flour and water paste and use it as a substitute. The composition will not be so strong, but at least it will not be potentially harmful. A recipe for flour and water paste follows this paragraph. Lastly, oil of cloves can be purchased or ordered at most drug stores.

Recipe for Flour and Water Paste

To make flour and waste paste, bring 1 cup of water to boil in a small saucepan. In another container stir 3 tablespoons of flour and ⅓ cup of cold water

5-1 Cooking torn paper.
Photograph by
Mary A. Salmon

5-2 Rinsing cooked paper.
Photograph by
Mary A. Salmon

to a smooth consistency. Pour the flour and water into the boiling water. Stir until it thickens. Pour the paste into a disposable container (like an aluminum-foil pie tin). Stir a drop or two of oil of cloves or a teaspoon of Clorox into the paste to prevent it from souring or molding. Allow the paste to cool before you use it. The paste can be stored one or two days in the refrigerator.

To begin making a batch of Recipe I composition, tear the magazine and kraft paper into bits no larger than ½ x ½ inch. Place the paper pieces in a large enameled pot such as a waterbath canner. Do not use aluminum. The alkali in the paper will corrode aluminum. Tear, never cut, the paper into small pieces. We are returning the paper to its previous pulp state—a mass of fibers. These fibers will bond together again with the other ingredients to form the composition. The longer the fibers, the stronger the composition. Cutting chops up and shortens the fibers, whereas tearing only pulls them apart.

Cover the paper bits with water and add two tablespoons of household bleach to the pan. Place the mixture on the stove and bring it to a boil. Reduce the heat, cover the pan, and simmer the contents for two hours. Stir from time to time. Cooking further reduces the paper to pulp and the bleach removes most of the color. The odor of the simmering paper is unusual, but not harmful.

Next, place a colander or large strainer in the sink. Remove the pan of cooked paper from the stove. The pan contains globs of mushy paper floating in an unpleasantly colored broth. Pour the mixture into the colander and let it drain. Rinse the cool paper mass with water until the liquid running from the colander is clear. Return the paper mass to the pan.

Now, the paper must be beaten. This process should whip the paper with such force that it separates any remaining pieces into pulp and even individual fibers. A kitchen blender will accomplish this task nicely. If you use sufficient water, the blender will be none the worse for wear. Place the colander or strainer in the sink again and line it with a piece of cheesecloth. Place a lump of wet paper about the size of a plum in the blender. Fill the blender with water. First chop and then blend the paper for one minute. Turn off the blender. Pour its contents into the cheesecloth-lined drainer. If you don't have a blender, beat the paper briskly by hand with a metal whisk.

Have a disposable container waiting nearby. If you buy milk in plastic gallon jugs, cut off the top half of the jug and use the bottom half as a container (these also make excellent containers for mixing plaster). Next, lift the cheesecloth above the strainer, gathering the corners to prevent dumping the paper pulp. Gently squeeze out some of the water. Do not overdo this step. The pulp should be almost 90 percent water for it to be a pliable modeling compound. If too much of the water is removed from the pulp, the resulting composition will be lumpy and difficult to work with. This is a gray area; only as you gain experience will you recognize when pulp has the correct moisture content. Continue with the processes of beating and squeezing until all the pulp is in the disposable container.

5-3 Beating cooked paper.
Photograph by Mary A. Salmon

Add to the container all the other ingredients except the dry wheat wall-paper paste. If you are using flour and water paste, it can be added now. Mix thoroughly. Sprinkle the wallpaper paste over the mixture. Stir it into the other ingredients and the composition is ready to be used.

To store, put the container of composition into a plastic bag. Seal the bag tightly. Place it in the refrigerator. Composition can be kept refrigerated for several weeks. However, each time it is taken out of the bag and exposed to the air for any period of time, it becomes dryer and consequently more difficult to use.

Recipe II

Recipe II produces enough composition to make the heads, arms, legs, and torsos of both Hansel and Gretel (Project Three). Composition was pressed into sized plaster molds to form the parts of the dolls. They stand 9 inches tall. The circumference of their heads is 5 ½ inches.

Materials

½ roll of good quality white toilet paper
4 tablespoons of white glue
1 tablespoon of raw linseed oil
2 tablespoons of wheat wallpaper paste or ¼ cup of
    flour and water paste
2 drops of oil of cloves or 1 tablespoon of Clorox

Measure, tear, cook, beat, and mix the ingredients of Recipe II following the same instructions for preparing composition from Recipe I.

Recipe III

This recipe produces ½ cup of modeling compound. It provides a quick substitute for Recipes I and II. Use it for repairs or small additions to a finished surface, but I would not recommend the mixture for an entire head.

Materials

2 slices of bread
2 tablespoons of white glue
2 drops of glycerine or 2 drops of liquid detergent

Remove crusts from the bread and crumble the slices into a small container. Add white glue such as Elmer's to the bread. Add glycerine (which can be purchased or ordered from most drug stores) or liquid detergent to the bread and glue. Knead the mixture until it is no longer sticky and it is ready to use. This modeling compound can be stored for weeks in the refrigerator in a plastic bag or covered jar.

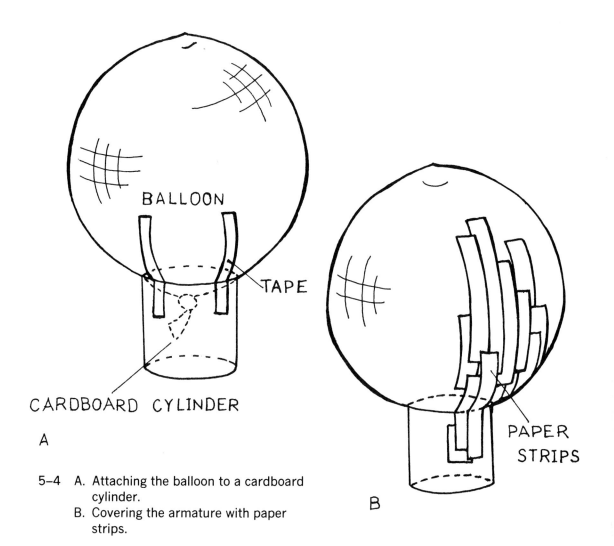

BALLOON

TAPE

CARDBOARD CYLINDER

A

5-4   A. Attaching the balloon to a cardboard
         cylinder.
      B. Covering the armature with paper
         strips.

PAPER
STRIPS

B

APPLIED COMPOSITION

Dolls made of applied composition are one of a kind. An armature, which need not be permanent, is constructed. Over its surface is applied a layer of wet composition. When dry, the doll head is hard and durable, and the armature is no longer necessary to hold the shape. This method is suited to the individual dollmaker who is interested in making single dolls with a minimum of fuss and investment.

STEP I: *The Armature.* A large percentage of the wet composition modeling compound is water. It will not hold the shape of a doll head or limbs without support. An armature supplies support. It is constructed following the basic contours of the object to be modeled.

An excellent armature for a doll's head is a small round balloon. The balloon is inflated to slightly less than the circumference of the finished head. A section of a cardboard cylinder (such as is found inside a roll of aluminum foil or paper towels) is slipped over the knotted end of the balloon and taped in place with masking tape (fig. 5-4A). If you are making a very small head it will be necessary to cut open the cardboard cylinder and roll it tighter. When you have achieved the correct diameter for the neck, tape it closed.

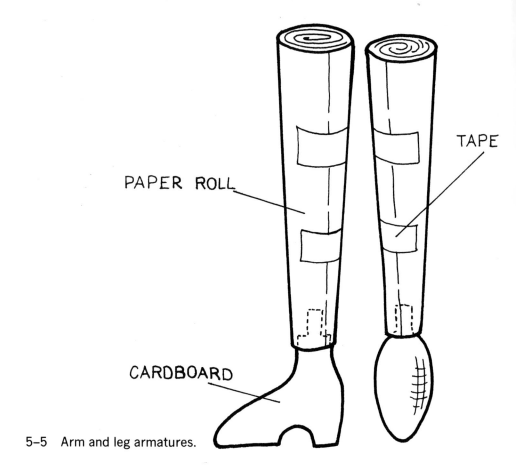

PAPER ROLL

TAPE

CARDBOARD

5–5 Arm and leg armatures.

To make simple armatures for the arms and hands, legs and feet, use a combination of rolled newspaper and cardboard cutouts (fig. 5-5). Roll strips of newspaper into tight forms the length of the proposed arm from wrist to elbow and the leg from ankle to knee. The rolls should be cylindrical and broader at elbow or knee end. Tape the forms so they will not unroll. From a sheet of lightweight cardboard cut basic hand and foot (or boot) shapes with tabs to insert into the rolls of newspaper. For example, the hand can be a spoon shape with a tab on the wrist end (fig. 7-3). Coat the tab with white glue. Insert the tab into the center of the narrow end of the newspaper roll. Repeat this procedure, gluing a hand or foot shape to each roll.

STEP 2: *Fortifying the Armature.* Wet composition is heavy. The armatures I have described would collapse under the weight of the wet mixture. An additional step is necessary to make the armatures sturdy. Three layers of narrow strips of paper dipped into paste are applied over the surface of the balloon, newspaper, and cardboard.

To begin, refer back to Recipe I composition and make a batch of flour and water paste following the recipe in that section. While the paste cools, tear two pages of newspaper into strips measuring approximately ½ x 1 inch. Dip one strip into the cooled paste. When it is thoroughly saturated, remove it. Run the paper strip between two fingers to draw off any excess paste. Press the strip to the armature and smooth it against the surface. Repeat this procedure, covering the entire surface of each armature with a smooth overlapping layer of paste impregnated paper strips (fig. 5-4B).

The paper strips should be dry before an additional layer is applied. They will dry overnight or in a few hours if placed near (but not on) a heat duct or radiator.

Next, apply a layer of strips of paper torn from a brown paper bag. The change of color will assure a total cover. Allow this layer time to dry.

Just prior to applying the last layer of paper strips, it is important to build up portions of the armatures. This procedure causes the armatures to more closely resemble the structure of the objects they are to become, but it also makes possible an even application of composition. If you waited to shape the features with composition, some areas would require a much thicker layer than the overall surface. Composition becomes unusually bumpy and can warp if it dries unevenly. Equal drying time is promoted by keeping the composition layer of uniform thickness.

Areas that require building are cheeks, chin, nose, ears, forehead, back of the head, hands, and feet. Coat these areas with diluted white glue (two parts glue to one part water). Tightly crumble small pieces of newspaper into wads the size of a pea. Glue groups of these wads on the surface of the armature to give shape to forms with bulk (fig. 5-6). A folded strip of thin cardboard can be glued to the armature to serve as a support for the nose. Cover these additions as well as all remaining surfaces of the armatures with a last layer of overlapping strips of newspaper dipped in paste. When dry, the armature is sufficiently sturdy to accept a layer of composition.

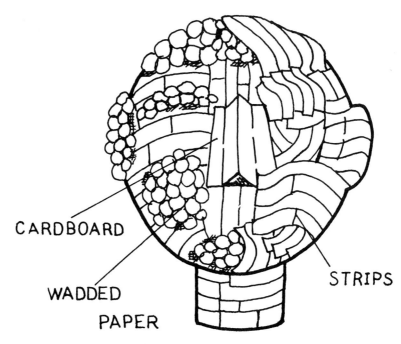

CARDBOARD

WADDED

PAPER

STRIPS

5–6   Building forms on the surface of the armature.

STEP 3: *Applying Composition.* Before beginning to apply composition, it is a good idea to have the armature firmly fixed in one position. Handling the armature as you work would damage the modeling. An inexpensive plastic turntable (available at most grocery and department stores) serves this purpose nicely. A plate or small board placed on a smooth work surface will also suffice. Put a wad of plastiline (oil-based clay) in the center of the plate, turntable, or board. Push the base of the neck of the head, leg, or arm armature into the clay so it is held securely in position. Scrape the clay away from the outside of

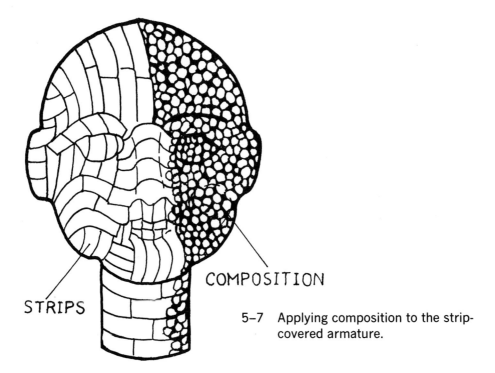

STRIPS

COMPOSITION

5–7 Applying composition to the strip-covered armature.

the armature until it overlaps by only ⅛ to ¼ inch. The armature can now be rotated by moving the surface to which it is affixed. It is possible to apply composition to all sides without touching finished areas.

To proceed, coat the entire outside surface of the armature with a light application of white glue and water (two parts glue to one part water). While the surface is still wet, begin to apply a layer of composition. You can use your fingers or a palate knife. Press the modeling compound in a thin, uniform layer to cover the entire exposed surface of the armature. This is the first of two layers. Set the armature aside until the first layer is dry (refer to Step 4: *Drying Applied Composition*).

When the first layer is dry, again coat the surface with diluted glue. Apply the second and last layer of composition. Aim for the two layers to produce a ⅜- to ½-inch composition shell. The second layer should be carefully modeled. (Chapter Nine, Bisque, discusses modeling and tools in detail; the same principles apply to composition.) Use fingers, clay modeling tools, or any convenient article to produce the desired shape and texture of the doll's skin and features.

STEP 4: *Drying Composition.* As composition dries, it shrinks. Regardless of how smooth the surface was at the onset of the drying process, it will become bumpy. Fortunately, each successive layer dries smoother, and, when composition has lost most of its moisture, it remains plastic. At this point, the surface can be made smooth and it will retain this smoothness when it is dry.

The first thin layer of composition applied to the armature will dry overnight. This process can be expedited by placing the object near a heat vent or in a warm (150°) oven. Composition will scorch, so if you use the oven, monitor the drying process closely. Do not worry about the surface texture of the first layer of composition.

When drying the second layer pay more attention to keeping the surface smooth. This will save time sanding and rasping later. Use your fingers or a knife to smooth the composition when it is almost dry.

At this point, make six holes with an awl or a drill 1½ inches above the base of the neck and equally spaced around its circumference (fig. 6-16). These are necessary when attaching the head to a fabric body.

Finishing the dry composition surface is discussed at a later point in this chapter.

MAKING A PLASTER MOLD FOR COMPOSITION

Another method used to force composition to retain a shape until it dries is to press the wet compound into a sized plaster mold. The composition will harden and dry, reproducing the shape of the mold. The prototype for the molded composition doll is modeled of oil-based clay. The mold is made from this model.

Molds have been part of the dollmaker's craft for centuries. Once a model has been designed, perfected, and cast, a mold makes possible perfect reproduction of the same doll over and over again. When dollmaking became big business in the early 1800s, it was common for two types of molds of the same doll to be in use. The original mold of a doll was called the "master" mold. The second mold was made from the master mold and was called a "pouring" mold. Factories used the pouring mold for the actual business of dollmaking. Approximately fifty heads could be formed in a pouring mold before it was worn out. The first doll poured in the mold was always the sharpest. Each successive doll showed less clear detail. The worn-out molds were discarded and new molds made from the master mold.

Molds made of simple doll parts generally have two pieces. These spherical forms must be divided at their widest points to produce the parts of a mold. The problem of determining where the widest points occur is a complicated one. Companies have specialized in the past and still do specialize in just mold-making. Have you ever set a marble in wet plaster and, after the plaster dried, tried to remove the marble? If it sank into the plaster below the point of its center, it was trapped and could not be removed without breaking the plaster. The widest point of the marble was below the edge of plaster and the opening that remained was too small to permit passage of the marble. An undercut was created. An undercut is a point at which a mold is wider than its opening. An undercut will cause damage to the finished piece when an attempt is made to remove it from the mold. For more complicated dolls, molds of several pieces have to be designed. Determining the point of division and the direction of the movement of the mold away from the cast doll is a problem defined as "draft." For purposes of this book, two-piece molds of relatively simple forms are encouraged. A brief description of a three-piece mold of a cupped hand appears in Chapter Thirteen.

Molds for dolls can be made of a number of materials. Metal and plaster are examples. The mold material must sharply retain the details of the model and pass these details on to the casting compound. Plaster is ideally suited to the purposes of the individual dollmaker. It is inexpensive and easy to use and produces molds of long life. Buy a good quality of plaster. I recommend potter's plaster. Plaster purchased at hardware stores is not suitable. Sources of supply for potter's plaster are listed at the end of the text. To maintain the quality of plaster, always store it in an airtight container.

Another point to be considered when planning to make a doll mold is whether or not the compound to be cast will form a bond with the plaster, preventing separation from the mold. To avoid this, some molds are sized. They are coated with a substance that reacts with neither the surface of the mold nor the material to be cast. The size keeps the two materials in close contact but separate. Plaster molds intended for use with composition are sized. They are painted with two thin coats of orange shellac. An end result of coating the mold with shellac is that the surface of the mold becomes impervious to moisture. Plaster aids in drying pieces cast in materials like porcelain because it absorbs moisture from the slip. Quick removal of the piece from the mold is feasible. This is not the case when molding composition. The pieces must be left to dry in the mold. This process may take two or three days, depending on humidity and the depth of the composition layer.

With this general information in mind, we are ready to proceed with the specific task of making a plaster mold.

STEP 1: *Designing a Prototype.* It is important when designing a doll to consider the methods and materials to be used for its production. In this case, a mold is to be made from the doll. If this is your first mold, simplicity is of the essence. Intricate details and curvaceous projections from the surface of the figure will cause undercuts and headaches. Keep the model sleek, streamlined, simple.

If you plan to make a head, torso, and limbs, another point to be considered is a system of joining the pieces of the doll together. Stationary head and limbs are simply glued into the sockets of the torso. But, if the parts of the doll are to be mobile, provisions for stringing elastic cord from limb to limb will have to be made. Refer to the dolls, Hansel and Gretel (Project Three). Note the elementary system of jointing used. It is sturdy and allows for a wide range of movement. A more elaborate setup is displayed by the body of the Goose Girl (Project Six). Her bisque head is attached to a German ball-jointed body that was purchased from a doll-parts supplier.

Dolls have been jointed in a wide variety of ways over the centuries. Joints vary with the material. Stitching provides an adequate joint for a fabric body, ball joints work well on wooden and composition bodies. Stringing the pieces of the doll body together with elastic cord is an invention attributed to the Chinese. It is considered to be one of the great advances in the craft of dollmaking.

The system of jointing determines to some extent the shape of doll parts. Decide on a method suitable for the doll you are planning to make before proceeding to the next step: modeling.

STEP 2: *Modeling the Prototype.* Plastiline is an oil-based clay that does not harden. It is an excellent material out of which to model the doll to be cast. A good quality of plastiline is wonderfully pliable, a pleasure to work with. Also, if the clay is kept free of impurities it can be reused. I recommend Roma Plas-

5–8   Plastiline, turntable, and modeling tools.

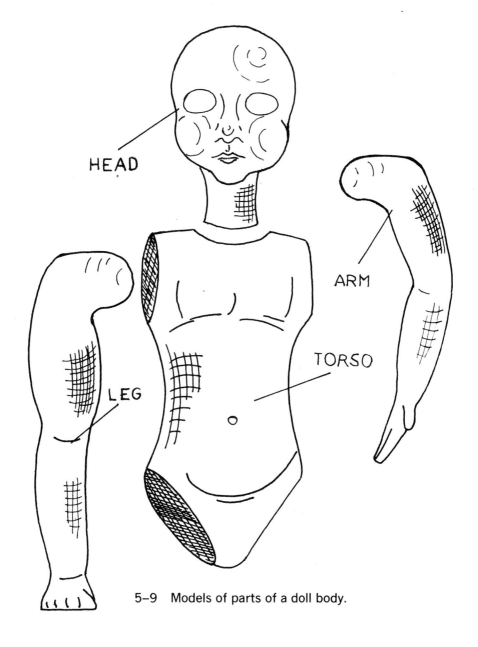

5-9   Models of parts of a doll body.

tilina #2. It can be purchased from art supply stores listed at the end of the text. Cheaper grades of plastiline, such as those recommended for schools, are less oily and, consequently, stiffer. Two pounds provides sufficient clay to model the head, torso, and limbs for a 9-inch doll such as Hansel or Gretel.

Prepare the plastiline by kneading lumps between your hands to make it soft and pliable.

To assure proper proportions, it is a good idea to simultaneously model all parts of the doll. Don't model the head, set it aside; then model the torso without referring back to the head. You may be unpleasantly surprised to find your memory was not so accurate as you imagined, and the body is larger or smaller in proportion to the head.

As you model, always be aware of areas that may cause undercuts. Any part of the model which protrudes wider than the center of the head can hold the model tightly in the plaster. A deep indentation in the model can draw plaster in and cause an undercut. Ears are also sometimes a problem. You can make a separate mold of the ears and glue them to the head after it comes from the mold, or you can model and apply composition ears to each individual dry head. Hands can be another touchy area. A cupped hand or separated fingers require extra care on the part of the mold maker. A hand with only a slight curve and subtle lines denoting fingers makes a successful mold.

Do not hollow out the areas of the torso designated to be neck, arm, and leg sockets. These areas will be cut out when the molded composition is almost dry. Do check to be sure that the base of the neck and the arms and the legs will fit into their proper spaces when they are cut out.

Model each individual doll part to represent, as accurately as possible, the design you have conceptualized. Hold your work up to a mirror and inspect your progress from different angles, in different degrees of light. If there are flaws in structure or proportion, these "tricks" will sometimes make the errors more visible.

Model plastiline plugs, shaped like corks, which will extend from the base of each model to the edge of the molds (fig. 5-10). The plugs provide channels, permitting air to enter the mold and aid drying the composition.

Lastly, smooth the surface of your work. Dipping your finger in water and rubbing the surface of the model works well on oil-based clay. It results in a highly satisfactory degree of smoothness for those areas representing skin.

When you are satisfied with each individual piece of your model and with the appearance of the pieces as a group, you are ready to go on to Step 3 and divide the pieces with shims.

STEP 3: *Shims.* There is more than one way to form a separation or seam line on a model, prior to pouring a two-piece mold. One way, discussed in detail in Chapter Thirteen, is to build up a wall of clay. Oil clay is used for the wall if the model is water clay, and a water clay wall is built if the model is oil clay. Another method commonly used is to make a wall of shims. Shims can be cut from metal or plastic. They are pressed into the clay of the model and form a barricade to hold back the plaster. They create a dividing point for the mold. Shims can be used only if the model is soft enough for them to penetrate its surface.

Figure 5-10 shows the head, torso, arm, and leg of Hansel divided with shims. Cut flat pieces, approximately 1 x 3 inches (the size of the shim will vary with the size of the doll part) from disposable aluminum freezer containers or plastic bottles.

Now, carefully survey the parts of the doll. Each piece should be divided along an imaginary line at their widest point. Some dollmakers drape a piece of string over the object. When the string is drawn tight it cuts into the widest parts of the model, leaving an identation in the clay along which to place the shims. Another method requires a sheet of carbon paper and a straightedge, such as a ruler. Lay the plastiline model on a flat surface positioned as it will be in the mold. Place the printing side of a sheet of carbon paper against the model. With one end of the ruler on the flat surface, slide the opposite end over the carbon paper. Trace the entire outline of the model with the end of the ruler. Keep the carbon between it and the surface of the clay. The widest points of the model will be clearly marked with carbon. Use these points as a guide when determining the dividing line for shim placement.

Once you have decided where to divide the piece, carefully mark the line on the model with a pointed tool. The line should encircle the piece including the plug (except for its base), dividing it into nearly equal halves. Insert the shims into the clay along the line. Push them deeply enough into the plastiline to be sturdlly fixed in place. The edge of one shim must be in tight contact with the

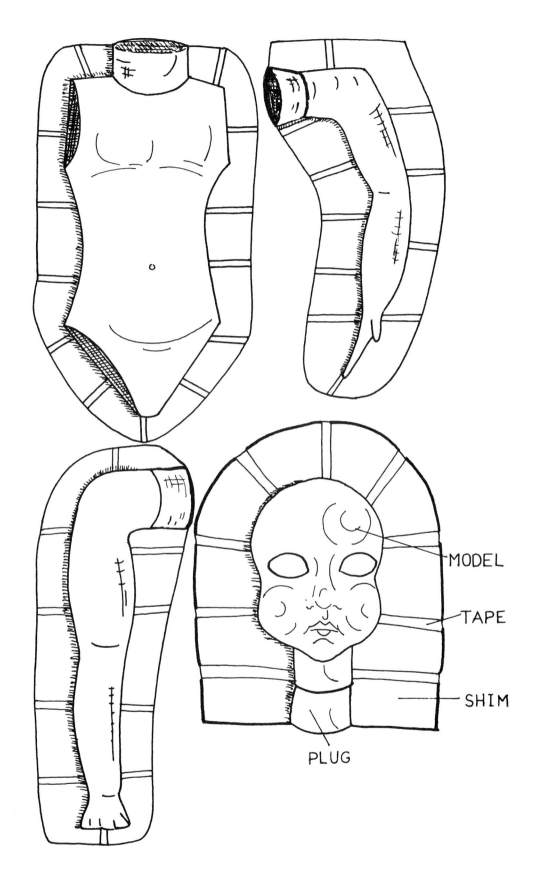

MODEL

TAPE

SHIM

PLUG

5-10 Dividing the models with shims.

edge of the next shim. Cover each joint with masking tape. This will prevent plaster from leaking between shims.

STEP 4: *Retaining Walls.* When plaster is poured over a model, some method must be employed to hold the liquid in place until it hardens. A traditional method, using mold boards and resulting in a square or rectangular mold, is discussed in Chapter Thirteen. The method that follows employs a nest, constructed of newspaper or fabric, to support the shims. The plaster is allowed to thicken and is then built up, rather than poured, over the model. The result is a round mold.

To make a nest, grasp each end of a sheet of newspaper or a rectangle of fabric and twist. Curl the twisted piece into a circle (fig. 5-11A). The circle should be slightly larger than the perimeter of the shims of the piece to be nested. Tape, tie, or tuck the ends of the twisted circle in place. Lay the model in the nest. Check to be sure the shims are well supported and level. The model and shims must be firmly supported or they will collapse under the weight of the plaster (fig. 5-11B).

Following these instructions, nest each plastiline model from which you plan to make a mold. Place the nested pieces on a flat work surface that has been protected with newspaper or plastic in case of accidental plaster spills or leaks.

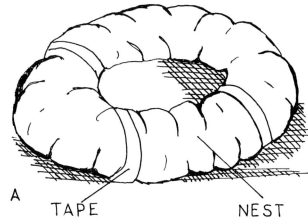

A   TAPE   NEST

5–11 A. Making a cloth or paper nest.
      B. Bedding the model in the nest.

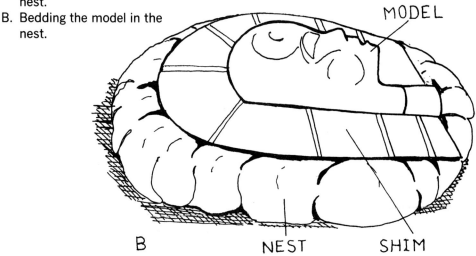

MODEL

B   NEST   SHIM

5-12 Mixing plaster.

STEP 5: *Mixing Plaster*. Plaster is messy! Protect your work area, including the floor, by covering it with a layer of newspaper or a drop cloth. Plaster also plugs drains. *Never* pour plaster into a sink. Mix plaster in disposable containers (for example, cut the bottom half from a plastic gallon milk jug) or use plastic bowls and allow the plaster to harden before cracking the leftover plaster into the garbage. Keep a bowl of water nearby in which to wash your hands (dispose of the water other than down a drain, after your work session is over).

The amount of plaster and the volume of water vary, depending on the kind of plaster you are using. These instructions are for potter's plaster.

Always add the plaster to the water. Never reverse this step. To begin (to make sufficient plaster for the first half of all six molds of the parts of one 9-inch doll), put 1 quart of water into a container. Measure out 3 pounds of plaster. One-half pound of plaster equals 1 cup. Be sure the measurements are accurate. Too little plaster to the ratio of water produces a soft crumbly mold, and too much plaster makes a mold that is dense and not absorbent (a consideration when casting clay slip). Now, carefully sift the plaster into the water by running it between your fingers, breaking up lumps. As you near completion, little mounds of plaster will begin to rise above the surface of the water. When all the plaster has been sifted into the water, leave the mixture to sit, undisturbed, for two to four minutes. This period, during which the plaster absorbs water, is called slaking. At the end of slaking, any water remaining on the surface of the plaster is poured off. Carefully pour the water into a disposable container.

Next, the plaster is stirred. You can use your hand, a dowel stick, or a spoon. It is important that the mixture be stirred slowly, steadily, back and forth from the bottom. This causes air bubbles to rise to the surface and break. Do not stir in a circular motion or whip the plaster. You will add air bubbles if you do. Gradually the plaster will begin to thicken. When it is the consistency of heavy cream it can be poured into a traditional mold. However, to build a cover over the models it must be thicker yet. When the plaster is no longer watery but is still plastic, it is ready to apply. This is called the cheese state.

STEP 6: *Pouring Plaster*. Plaster should be poured onto the surface of the models quickly, smoothly, but with a little force to explode any air bubbles. Do not, however, pour with such force it causes the plaster to splash. Build up the plaster in a uniform manner. It should be the same thickness over each part of the model. The surface of the mold will be uneven. Do not cover the base of the plugs. They should remain visible.

When you have poured the plaster over each piece, jar your work table two or three times. This will explode any lingering air bubbles near the surface of the model. To finish, dip a palette or butter knife into a jar of water and gently smooth the wet plaster surface of each mold.

Now, leave the plaster alone to set up. This is a process of crystallization during which the plaster gives off heat. As soon as it starts to cool, the physical change is complete. The plaster is hard. Setting up will take thirty to forty minutes.

Next, turn the pieces over and rest the plaster in the nest. Remove the shims from each model and gently smooth the plastiline to close any gaps left by their removal. Using a spoon, a knife, or a similarly shaped instrument, make keys. Keys are notches carved in the inside surface of the first half of the mold. When the second section of the mold is poured, plaster will flow into these indentations, forming knobs. The knobs fit into the notches locking the mold together. They assure the mold will close tightly and accurately. After you carve the keys, smooth their interior with fine sandpaper.

Although the models appear ready to accept pouring of the second half of the molds, if you did so now, the second batch of plaster would adhere solidly to the first. The surface of the first half of the mold, which will come in contact with the new plaster, must be sized. The size used to keep plaster layers from bonding is generally a soap and oil mixture. It can be purchased premixed from most sources of ceramic supply, some of which are listed in the back of the book. The liquid is called mold soap or mold release solution. For those of you who wish to make your own, recipes follow.

Mold Soap

Dissolve odds and ends of hand soap or castile soap in enough water to make a liquid soap the consistency of corn syrup (2 parts water/1 part soap). Add an equal amount of raw linseed oil. Mix.

or

Add ¼ cup of Fels Naptha or Ivory soap flakes (detergents will not do) to 2 cups of water. Simmer until clear. Add 2 cups of boiling water. Stir. Cool.

Either mixture can be stored at room temperature in a closed container.

Coat the exposed plaster surface of your molds with this mixture or with a purchased mold soap. It is not necessary to coat plastiline or the plaster beneath your model. Use a sponge to apply the solution. The dry sponge should be dipped in size, never in water. Apply one layer. Pick up any excess with a soft brush. Apply five coats in this manner. The surface will appear glossy and be nonabsorbent after this treatment. Soap size is not permanent; it loses its effectiveness after approximately half an hour.

Now, following exactly the previous instruction, mix the same amount of plaster and pour the second half of the molds.

Allow the new plaster sufficient time to set up. It will take longer to crystallize than the first section. In about an hour the molds will be cool.

Using a knife, gently trim away plaster which may have dripped over the mold seam. Carefully open the mold. Lift out your model. It should come easily from the mold. If the model is difficult to remove and tears or shows signs of scruff marks, you may have undercuts. Evaluate this situation carefully. If the problem is minor and can be repaired by sanding, do so. If not, you will be unable to remove your cast piece from the mold without damage. The section of the mold with the undercut is valueless. Throw it away, correct your model, and remake that section of the mold.

STEP 7: *Drying the Mold.* A mold is not ready to use until it is dry. Small molds like these will dry in three or four days. The process can be speeded up by placing a mold near a heat vent or in a low (200°) oven. Take care, if the mold becomes too hot to handle it can soften and crumble. One way to test a mold for dryness is to hold it against your cheek. If the plaster is cool, it is still damp.

Molds that are going to be used for composition must be permanently sized with orange shellac. Coat the inside surface and the mold edges with a thin coat. When the first coat of shellac is dry, apply a second thin coat. The mold is now impervious to moisture and not suitable for use with clay slip. When the second coat of shellac is dry the mold is ready for use.

STEP 8: *Pressing Composition into the Mold.* Gently smooth a thin layer of vaseline over the surface of the shellacked plaster. Avoid swirls or globs that will be reproduced on the surface of the doll. Now, the casting surface of each mold is covered with a uniform layer of composition (fig. 8-2). The pieces will be hollow.

The composition can be applied to the mold in one of two ways. You can press globs of composition into the molds with your fingers. Be sure to maintain a layer of uniform thickness (¼ to ⅜ inch in depth). Or, place a pad of newspapers on a flat surface. Put a wad of composition about the size of a small apple on the newspapers. Use a rolling pin and press the wad into a sheet approximately ⅜ inch thick. Cut a rectangle from the sheet larger than the casting area of the mold. Lay the sheet of composition over the mold. Gently, easing without tearing, press the composition against the inside surface of the mold. Trim away the excess overlapping the edges of the mold.

When both halves of the mold have received a layer of composition, clap them together. Hold them closed with thick rubber bands. Set the mold aside until the composition has dried sufficiently to be firm, but is still plastic. This will take one or two days. If you set the mold near a heat vent, the composition will dry more quickly.

Remove the pieces from the mold. They are still damp and very fragile. With a sharply pointed knife, such as an X-Acto knife, cut the neck, arm, and leg sockets in the torso. Use a drill or an awl and make a hole through the base of each limb for passage of elastic cord. If you plan set-in eyes, this is also the time to cut off the cap of the head and make eye sockets. Refer to the Snow Queen (Project Two) for diagrams and detailed instructions explaining this procedure.

FINISHING THE COMPOSITION SURFACE

Regardless of how they were formed, the dry composition doll parts will exhibit a surface of varying degrees of roughness. Obvious niches or other imperfections should be filled or repaired with wet composition. Be sure to coat the dry surface with diluted white glue before pressing the composition into place. When these areas are dry, the surface can be smoothed. If the surface is extremely rough, begin smoothing with a medium to coarse wood rasp. Smooth the surface as much as possible with this tool. Next, proceed to coarse sandpaper and work your way on down to fine sandpaper. Sand until you have achieved the desired degree of polish. (Don't put a lot of energy into smoothing the portion of the head to be covered by the wig.)

When the head is smoothed to your liking, the surface should be painted with gesso. Gesso further smooths the composition surface by filling any tiny imperfections and covering rough spots. Gesso is a mixture, usually white, that prepares a surface to accept paint by closing its pores and slowing the rate of absorption. This makes sure that the paint colors will retain their brilliance. I prefer acrylic gesso. It dries quickly, flat white, and hard. It is a perfect ground for acrylic paints, which I use to color the composition surface. Before I continue, here is a recipe for gesso (not acrylic) that you can make yourself.

Gesso

Place 1 cup of water in a jar equipped with a lid. Sprinkle 4 tablespoons of whiting (see Sources of Supply) over the surface of the water. Do not stir. Allow the mixture to slake for twenty minutes. Pour off the excess water. Add 2 tablespoons of white glue and 1 tablespoon of raw or boiled linseed oil. Stir. The mixture should be thick, like cream. If it is not, add more whiting.

The dry surface of the composition doll parts should be coated with two thin applications of gesso. Use a bristle brush that has soaked in water for several minutes. Remove excess water from the bristles on a cloth and proceed to paint the pieces with gesso. When the first coat is dry and hard, apply a second coat.

The composition dolls featured in this book have been colored with acrylic paints. Acrylics are durable, nonyellowing paints with great light-refracting power. They are produced in a wide variety of colors and can be intermixed to produce an immense range of tints and shades. When dry they produce a hard, moisture-proof surface that can be cleaned with soap and water. For the dolls, you will need titanium white, mars black, cadmium red medium, cadmium yellow medium, and cerulean blue. Other necessary colors can be obtained by mixing two or more of the above. If you are new at mixing colors, buy an inexpensive color wheel from the art-supply store. It is a handy aid that will tell you which colors to mix to achieve a specific color. Chapters Six, Seven, and Eight provide more detailed information on mixing colors for dolls. The paints, like the gesso, dry quickly and hard. Thin acrylic paint with water, never with turpentine. Wet paint can be removed with soap and water. An acrylic solvent for removing dry paint can be purchased at most art-supply stores.

Sable and bristle brushes are suitable for applying acrylic paints to the surfaces of dolls. More than one size and type of brush is desirable. A No. 3 or 4 bright bristle brush (fig. 5-13) is good for applying gesso or painting large areas of flesh. Two round sable brushes (000 and 0) and one stippling brush (long, round, no taper) are handy for features. Buy high quality brushes and take care of them. To check for a good point, gently swish the brush in a glass of water, then sharply stroke it downward through the air. Immediately check the bristles. If they have come together into a clean sharp point, you have a good brush. When you bring home a new brush, wash it thoroughly but gently with mild dishwashing detergent and water. Rinse out all the soap. This will remove loose bristles and any impurities. Soak the brushes in water for twenty minutes before use with acrylic products. Remove excess water on a lint-free cloth before dipping into paint, gesso, or varnish. Immediately after use, clean

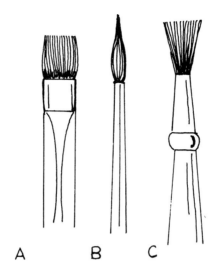

5–13 Brushes—A. Bright.
B. Round.
C. Stippler.

brushes thoroughly with mild soap and water. Rinse out the brushes and set them with bristles pointing upward to dry.

The painted surface of the composition doll can be given some additional protection against the ravages of time by applying a coat of acrylic varnish. Acrylic varnish is also water soluble when wet and dries quickly, hard, and transparent. It comes in two forms, gloss or matte. The gloss gives the undercoating of paint a shine, whereas matte assures a flat finish. One thin application of varnish brushed over all painted surfaces is sufficient. Do not allow the varnish to puddle in crevices. Puddles will dry opaque. When the varnish is dry, the doll is ready to be assembled and dressed.

Chapters Six, Seven, and Eight provide details for producing specific dolls of composition. Information on setting in eyes, making wigs, constructing fabric bodies, and assembling dolls is included, as are patterns for making complete outfits. Even if you are working on an original and do not plan to make the projects, read the chapters. They contain helpful information that is not presented elsewhere.

CHAPTER 6
Project One-Rumpelstiltskin

6-1   Rumpelstiltskin.

Today I bake, tomorrow I brew my beer;
The next day I will bring the Queen's child here.
Ah! Lucky 'tis that not a soul doth know
That Rumpelstiltskin is my name. Ho! Ho!
                                   The Brothers Grimm

The head of Rumpelstiltskin was formed by applying composition over a reinforced balloon-cardboard armature. It is attached to a jointed fabric body. The circumference of his head is 11½ inches. He is 18 inches tall. His hands are constructed of felt and pipe cleaners. The fingers bend and can hold objects. His clothing includes a knit sweater, stretch leotards, a corduroy jerkin, felt hat, felt shoes, and a money pouch.

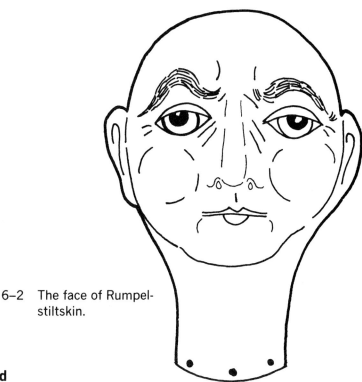

6–2   The face of Rumpel-
        stiltskin.

The Head

Before beginning work on the Rumpelstiltskin doll, read the portion of Chapter Five that discusses constructing an applied composition head. You will need the following materials for one head.

Materials

1 small round balloon
A 1½-inch section of cardboard cylinder with a
        diameter of 1½ inches
A batch of flour and water paste
Paper strips
White glue
½ of composition Recipe I
Acrylic gesso, paints, and varnish

Blow up the balloon until its circumference measures between 9 and 10 inches. Tape the knotted balloon to the cardboard cylinder (fig. 5-4A). Cover this armature with three layers of paper strips dipped in paste (fig. 5-4B), following the instructions outlined in Chapter Five. Be sure to build up necessary features before applying the last layer of strips (fig. 5-6). Cover the head with a thin layer of composition and allow it to dry (fig. 5-7). Add a second layer of composition. This will be the surface of the head, so model it carefully.

When the head is dry, punch (using an awl or drill) six evenly spaced holes around the circumference of the neck (fig. 6-16) ¼ inch above the base. These holes will be used to attach the head to the fabric body. Take care not to plug the holes when applying gesso, paint, and varnish.

Rasp and sand the head smooth.

Apply two thin coats of gesso, covering the composition surface. When the gesso is dry, mix acrylic paints, red, white, and a touch of yellow, arriving at a swarthy flesh color. Keep in mind, acrylics dry slightly darker than they appear wet. Paint the head and neck with this mixture.

When the first layer of paint on the head is dry, refer to figure 6-2. This is a close-up of Rumpelstiltskin's face. Use the drawing as a guide and lightly sketch (with a pencil) the features on the doll's head. Paint the eyebrows black. Outline the eye, upper lid, and iris with black. Paint the pupil black. Mix red, yellow, and blue to achieve brown and paint the iris brown. Mix red and white to arrive at a rosy pink. Paint the cheeks. Lightly rub a clean, soft cotton cloth over the cheeks to soften the color and blend it into the face. Apply pink to the end of the nose and center of the ear. Soften these areas with the cloth also. Mix red and yellow to make orange. Paint the mouth, nostrils, and the line denoting the ear lobe with this color. Use brown to paint the frown lines running from the corners of the eyes, mouth, and eyebrows and around the nose. Paint the white portion of the eye around the iris and place a dab of white paint in the center of each pupil for a highlight.

When the paint is dry, apply a coat of acrylic varnish. I prefer gloss varnish for a doll's head, but matte is equally suitable. It is a matter of taste.

The Wig and Beard

The illusion of hair on dolls has been created in a number of different ways. The most popular method has been to mold the hair directly on the head and color it with paint. The most popular fibers prior to the 1930s were human hair and mohair. There are any number of materials available to today's doll-maker for wigmaking: yarn, lamb's wool, pile, imitation fur fabrics, and cotton and silk embroidery thread, as well as those mentioned above. The fibers can be stitched to fabric creating a wig, or glued or inserted into tiny holes or a slit in the doll's head.

Rumpelstiltskin's wig is made of black Italian mohair yarn. Mohair yarn is woven from the fleece of an angora goat. It closely resembles human hair because of the long tendrils that stray from each woven strand. It also retains the animal oils, adding to the illusion. It comes in a wide variety of colors or it can be dyed to duplicate specific colors. It also can be curled. Mohair yarn is sold in 2-ounce skeins. A skein will make several wigs, depending, of course, on the size of the doll and the length of hair. Sources of supply for mohair yarn are listed at the back of the book. For small dolls, you can use mohair rovings. These individual fibers have not yet been woven into a strand. They can be purchased at weavers' supply stores. Also, mohair curls can be purchased from doll-parts suppliers. Natural or white mohair yarn, curls, or rovings can be dyed any hair color you envision with a human hair dye such as Clairol's Loving Care. A list of materials necessary to make Rumpelstiltskin's wig and beard follows.

Materials

Five yards of mohair yarn
A scrap of fabric (4 x 4 inches) matching the color
    of the yarn
White glue
Thread to match the yarn

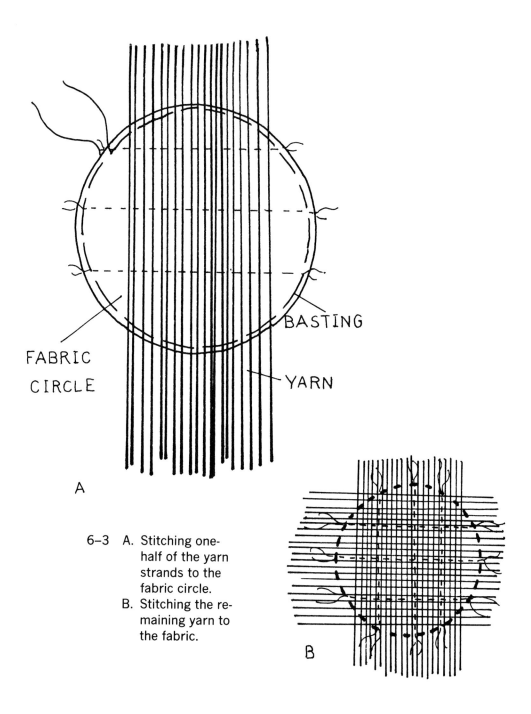

FABRIC
CIRCLE

BASTING

YARN

A

6–3 A. Stitching one-
half of the yarn
strands to the
fabric circle.
B. Stitching the re-
maining yarn to
the fabric.

B

To begin Rumpelstiltskin's wig, cut a circle of sturdy cotton fabric with a diameter of 4 inches. This is the wig patch that will be glued over the crown of
the doll's head. Baste around the circumference of this piece ¼ inch from the
edge. Leave the ends of the thread dangling so you can draw up the stitching
later.

Cut 5 yards of mohair yarn into 7-inch strands. Refer to figure 6-3A and lay
half of these strands in close contact with one another across the fabric circle.
Machine stitch the yarn to the fabric with three rows of thread. Arrange the remainder of the yarn at right angles to the first (fig. 6-3B). Stitch these strands
to the fabric. Draw up the basting stitches. The fabric circle will become a cup.
Adjust the gathers so the cup fits tightly over the crown of the doll's head.

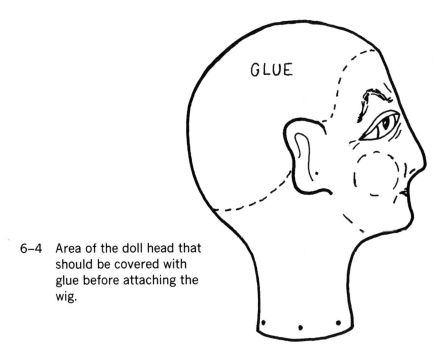

GLUE

6–4 Area of the doll head that
should be covered with
glue before attaching the
wig.

Paint the area of the doll's head, from which hair would grow, with a thin application of white glue. This area is larger than the wig patch (fig. 6-4). Press the wig in place. Use two or three rubber bands to hold the hair to the head until the glue dries.

When the glue is dry, cut the yarn, styling the hair. Rumpelstiltskin has short bangs in front and generally uneven, wild hair that accents his character. Save any mohair cuttings. They can be used for his beard.

Group fifteen mohair cuttings (approximately 1½ inches in length) tightly together. The ends of these pieces should be even. Coat an area (the size of a nickel) below the doll's lower lip with a thin application of white glue. Press the group of mohair cuttings against the glue. Put a rubber band around the head to hold the beard in place. Fan out and trim the ends of the beard when the glue is dry.

Hands

Each of Rumpelstiltskin's hands is constructed of two layers of felt between which are glued pieces of pipe cleaner. The pipe cleaners bend and hold the hand and fingers in a variety of positions. Twist ties, such as are used to keep plastic garbage bags closed, can be substituted for pipe cleaners.

Materials

One 9 x 12-inch rectangle of felt (in a color suitable
    for hands)
10 pipe cleaners or 10 twist ties
Fabric glue or liquid latex

6–5　Rumpelstiltskin's body.

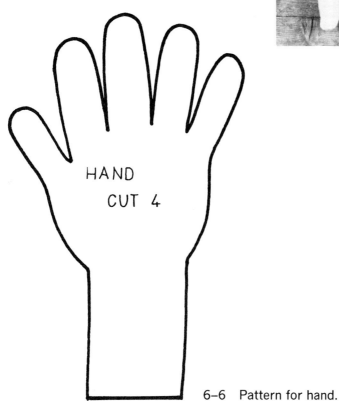

HAND

CUT 4

6–6　Pattern for hand.

Using the hand pattern (fig. 6-6), cut four felt pieces. Cut a piece of pipe cleaner the length of each finger from ⅛ inch within the fingertip to the wrist of the hand. Coat one felt piece with fabric glue or liquid latex. Place a pipe cleaner in the center of each glue-covered finger (fig. 6-12). Align and press the second felt hand-piece over the first, with the pipe cleaners sandwiched between. Repeat this procedure and assemble the second hand.

The Body

Rumpelstiltskin's torso and limbs are constructed from fabric. His body is jointed at the shoulder, hip, elbow, and knee. Lines of stitching serve as joints.

TORSO CUT 2

BASE CUT 1

6-7 Patterns for torso and base.

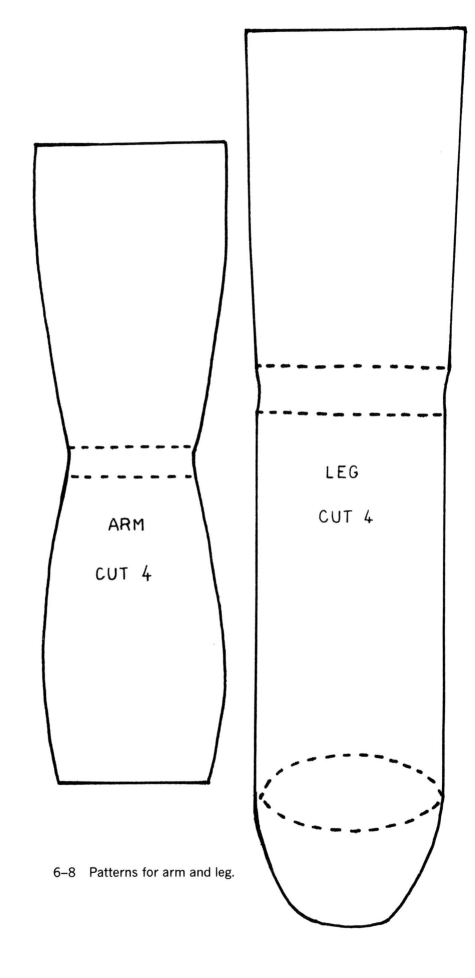

ARM

CUT 4

LEG

CUT 4

6–8 Patterns for arm and leg.

Materials

¼ yard of flesh-colored, sturdy cotton fabric (such
    as Kettle cloth)
Thread to match the fabric
¼ pound of polyester stuffing

Use the patterns (fig. 6-7, 6-8) as guides and cut arms, legs, base, and tor-so pieces from fabric. Cut the number of pieces marked on each pattern. Transfer the dotted stitching lines to the right side of the fabric.

To begin, stitch both sides of the torso pieces together from their base to the notches at the neck (fig. 6-9). Stitch the base to the lower edge of the body pieces (fig. 6-10). Turn the body right side out through the gap left between the two notches.

Stitch the long sides of each pair of arm pieces together, leaving both ends unstitched (fig. 6-11). Turn these pieces right side out.

To attach the hands to the arms, turn ¼ inch of fabric along the narrower, wrist end of one arm to the inside. Insert the wrist of a hand into the arm (fig. 6-13). Stitch the arm to the hand, placing the line of stitching ⅛ inch within the wrist of the arm. Assemble the second hand and arm.

The arms can now be stuffed. Using pea-sized wads of polyester stuffing, fill the lower arm from the wrist to within 1 inch of the dotted stitching lines that are marked for the elbow joint. The limbs should be soft and flexible when stuffed, not firm. Machine stitch, twice, over the dotted lines. Stuff the upper arm from the elbow joint to within 1 inch of the open end. Turn ¼ inch of fab-ric around the open edges to the inside and stitch the base of the arm closed. Repeat, assemble, and stuff the second arm.

Stuff the toe of one leg to within ½ inch of the curved dotted lines marked on the fabric. Then, take a tuck in the fabric, bringing the two dotted lines to-gether (fig. 6-14). Using small, concealed hand stitches, stitch the tuck closed. The tuck will bend the end of the leg upward, at right angles to the an-kle, and create a foot. Stuff the lower leg as you did the lower arm to within 1

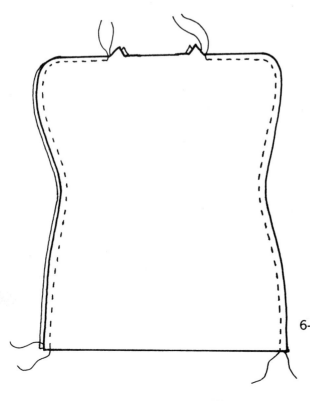

6–9   Stitching together the torso.

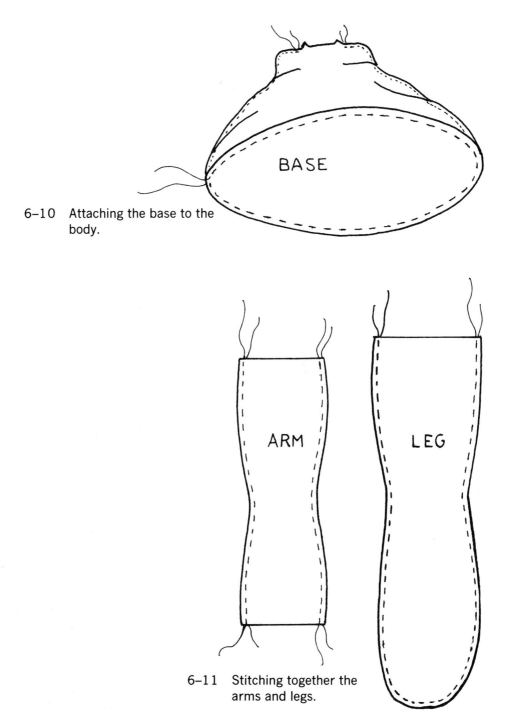

6-10 Attaching the base to the body.

6-11 Stitching together the arms and legs.

inch of the dotted stitching lines marked at the knee. Stitch over these lines twice. Stuff the leg to within 1 inch of the base of the leg. Turn ¼ inch of fabric to the inside and stitch the leg closed. Repeat, creating a foot and finishing the second leg.

Stuff the torso. Begin by placing a pad of stuffing in the base and working your way upward. The eraser end of a pencil or the blunt end of an aluminum crochet hook makes a good tool for pushing stuffing into hard-to-reach areas. Stuff the torso firmer than the limbs. The finished surface should be resilient

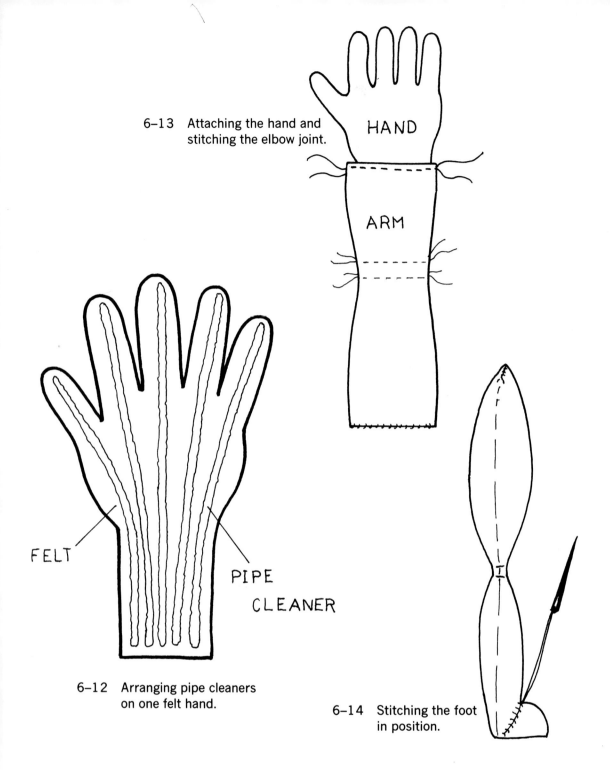

6–13 Attaching the hand and stitching the elbow joint.

HAND

ARM

FELT

PIPE

CLEANER

6–12 Arranging pipe cleaners on one felt hand.

6–14 Stitching the foot in position.

to the touch, but don't strain the seams by overstuffing. Leave enough of a gap in the stuffing to insert the neck of the head ½ inch into the opening between the notches.

Turn ¼ inch of fabric around the neck edge of the torso to the inside. Cut six 6-inch strands of embroidery thread, nylon cord, or a similar sturdy twine. In-

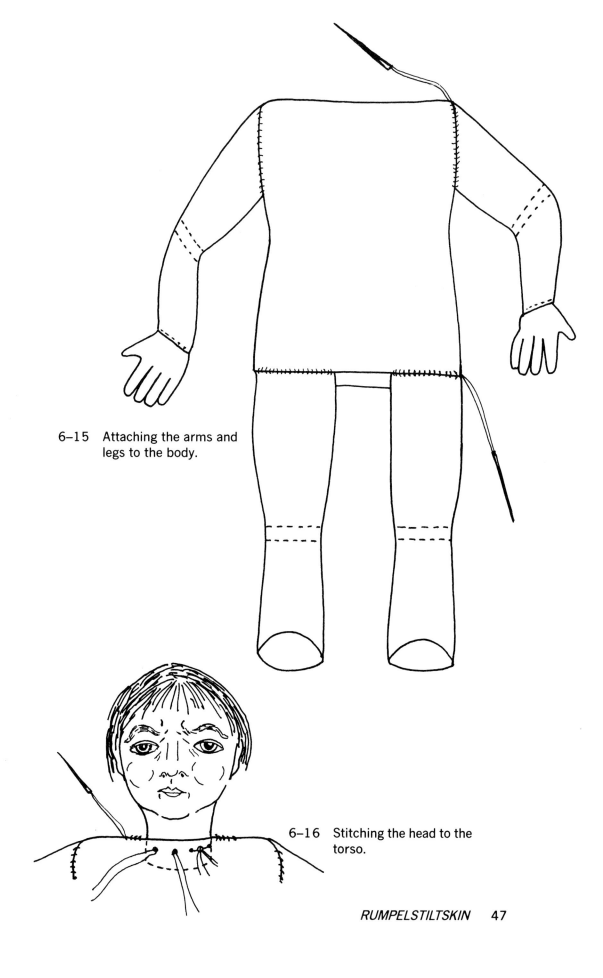

6–15 Attaching the arms and legs to the body.

6–16 Stitching the head to the torso.

sert two lengths of twine (from the inside out) into each pair of holes (fig. 6-16) in the base of the head. Two pieces of twine should be left dangling from each hole. Insert the neck into the body. Stitch the ends of each strand of twine through the fabric of the body (fig. 6-16). Do not pull them out of the head. When all pieces have been drawn to the outside, tie each pair in a sturdy knot. Trim the ends. Place a drop of glue on each knot to prevent its coming untied. Stitch the shoulders of the torso together so it fits snugly around the neck.

Firmly stitch each arm to the side of the torso at shoulder level (fig. 6-15). Thumbs should be pointing away from the body. Stitch a leg to each side of the base of the front of the torso with the toes pointing toward the front (fig. 6-15).

The doll is assembled and ready to dress.

Clothing

Rumpelstiltskin's clothing consists of a brown corduroy jerkin tied at the waist with a crocheted black rug-yarn belt. His sweater is made of gray knit fabric that was cut from an old sweater. The yellow leotards were cut from an outgrown pair of girl's leotards. The shoes and hat are felt. His money pouch is crushed velvet.

Materials

¼ yard of fabric for the jerkin
3 yards of rug yarn for the belt
¼ yard of knit fabric for the sweater
A 9 x 12-inch rectangle of felt for the hat
A piece of stretch nylon fabric (14 x 14 inches) for
    the leotards
A 6 x 8-inch piece of felt for the shoes
A scrap of fabric measuring 8 x 8 inches for the
    money pouch
A 10-inch length of ¼-inch-wide elastic
Thread to match the fabrics

Use the patterns (fig. 6-17, 6-18, 6-19) as a guide and cut the desired number of pieces from the fabrics you have chosen. Cut a rectangle of fabric measuring 4½ x 20 inches for the skirt of the jerkin. Cut a rectangle of sweater fabric measuring 3 x 9 inches for the collar of the sweater. Cut two rectangles of fabric measuring 3½ x 5½ inches for the money pouch. Transfer all markings to the wrong side of the fabric pieces.

LEOTARDS. To begin, we will make the leotards. With right sides together, stitch from the tip of one toe to the waist edge (fig. 6-20). Turn ½ inch of fabric along the waist edge to the inside. Stitch close to the turned edge of the fabric to create a casing for the elastic waistband (fig. 6-21). Thread a 10-inch length of ¼-inch elastic through the casing, stitching it securely to both ends of the casing. Stitch the opposite leg together from the toe to the waist. Stitch the crotch seam. Turn the leotards right side out and put them on the doll.

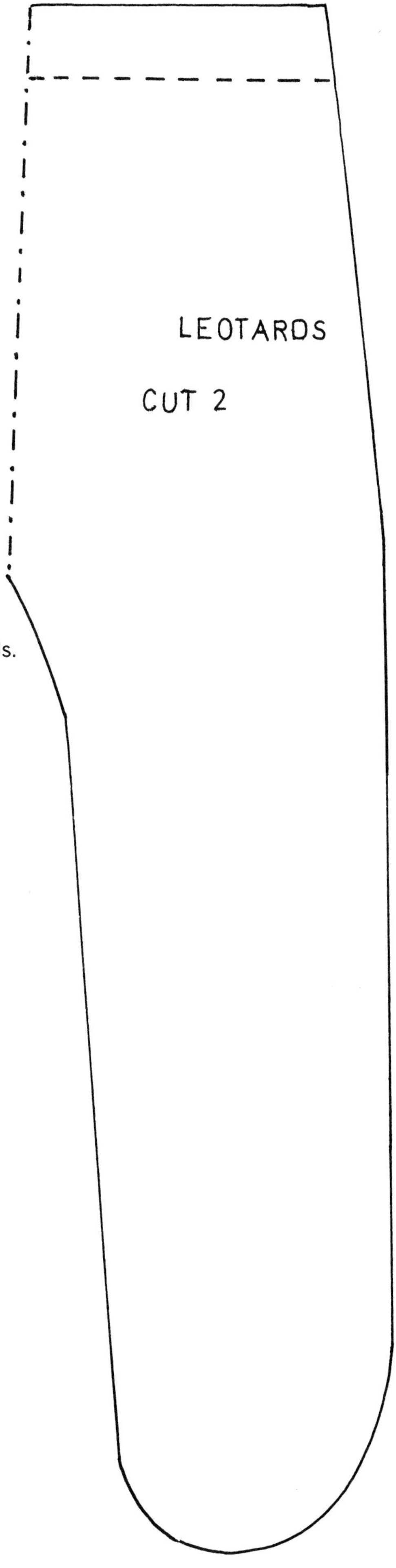

LEOTARDS

CUT 2

6-17   Pattern for leotards.

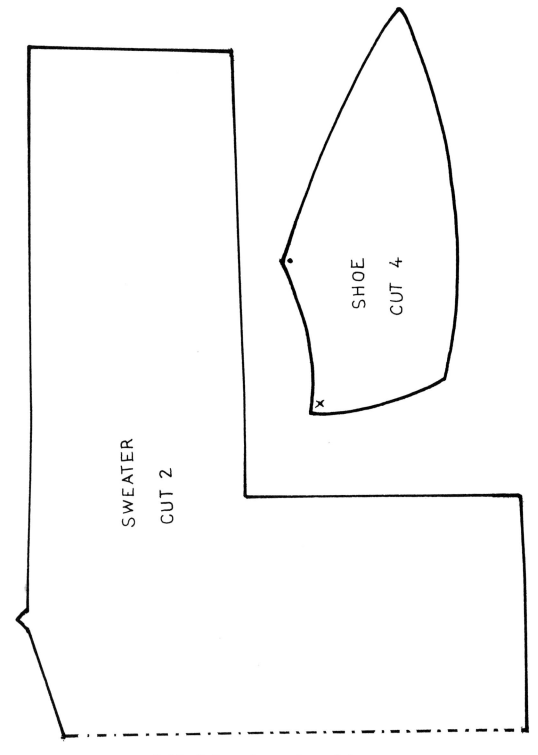

SWEATER
CUT 2

SHOE
CUT 4

6–18   Patterns for sweater and shoes.

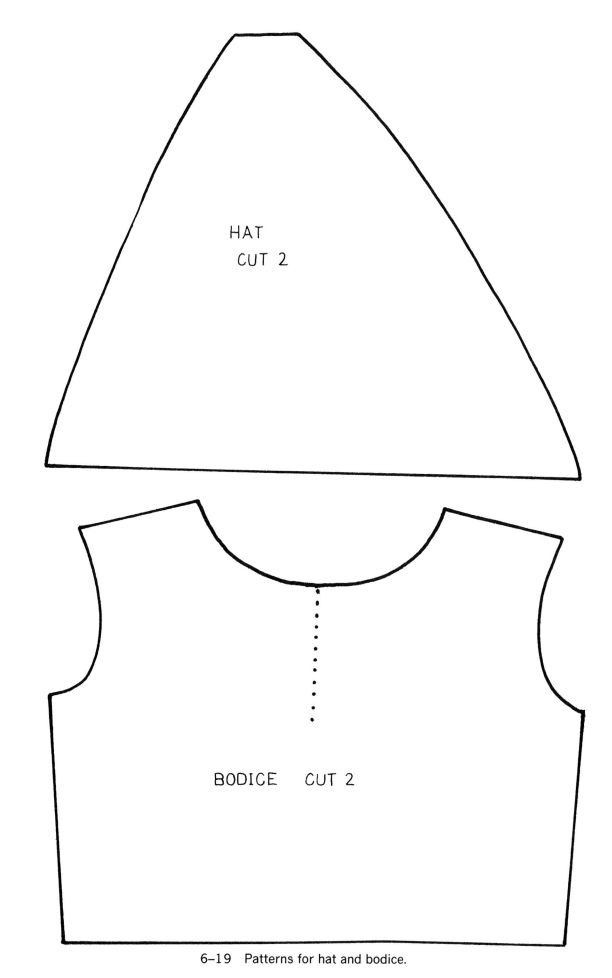

HAT
CUT 2

BODICE   CUT 2

6-19   Patterns for hat and bodice.

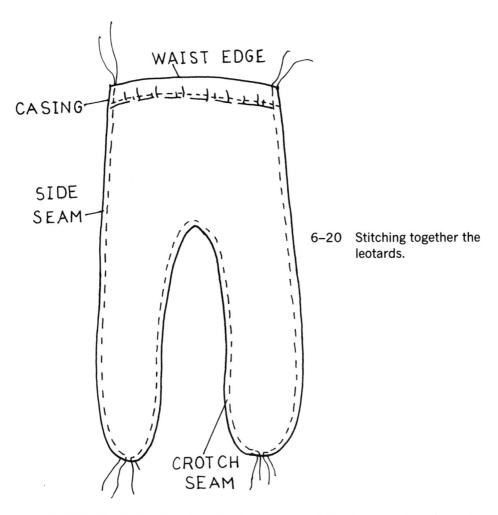

WAIST EDGE

CASING

SIDE
SEAM

CROTCH
SEAM

6–20   Stitching together the leotards.

SWEATER. Next, stitch the shoulder seams of the two sweater pieces together from the wrist edge to the notch (fig. 6-22). Stitch the underarm seams from the base of the sweater to the wrist ends of the sleeves. Hem the ends of the sleeves and the base of the sweater. Fold (in half the long way) the rectangle of fabric that is to be the collar of the sweater (fig. 6-23A). Stitch the short ends of the piece together. Turn it right side out and press. Put the body of the sweater on the doll. Wrap the collar around his neck with the stitched ends coming together at the back. Hand stitch the short ends of the collar together. Turn ¼ inch of the neck of the sweater to the inside. Tuck the base of the collar inside the neck edge of the sweater. Stitch the collar to the sweater, using small concealed hand stitches (fig. 6-23B).

JERKIN. To begin the jerkin, stitch together the shoulders of the bodice. Stitch the underarm seams. Cut a slit along the dotted lines marked on one bodice piece. This will be the front. Hem the neck edge, the front opening edges, and the armhole edges. To attach the skirt to the bodice, begin by stitching a line of basting ¼ inch within one long edge of the rectangular piece of skirt fabric. Turn ¼ inch of fabric along the opposite long edge to the inside. Press and stitch this edge in place. A decorative stitch and contrasting color of thread can be used to accent this hem. Stitch the narrow ends of the rectangle together. Next, draw up the basting thread so that the unhemmed edge of the skirt is gathered. With right sides together, pin the gathered edge of the skirt to the lower edge of the bodice. Baste and stitch the skirt to the bodice (fig. 6-24). Press. The jerkin is finished. After you put it on the doll, crochet a chain of rug yarn that will fit around his waist. Knot the ends. Tie it around the doll for a belt.

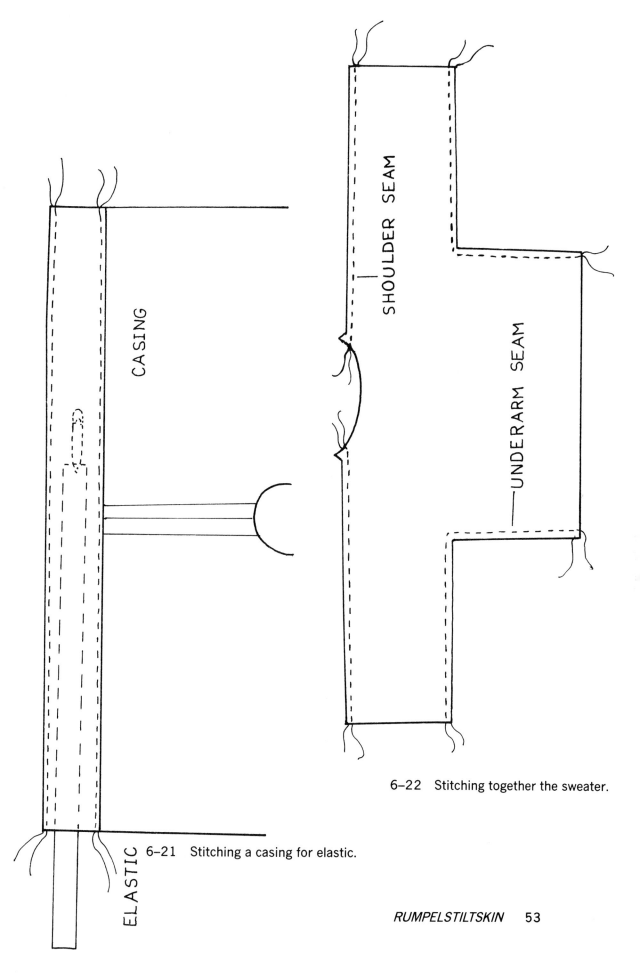

CASING

ELASTIC

6-21   Stitching a casing for elastic.

SHOULDER SEAM

UNDERARM SEAM

6-22   Stitching together the sweater.

RUMPELSTILTSKIN   53

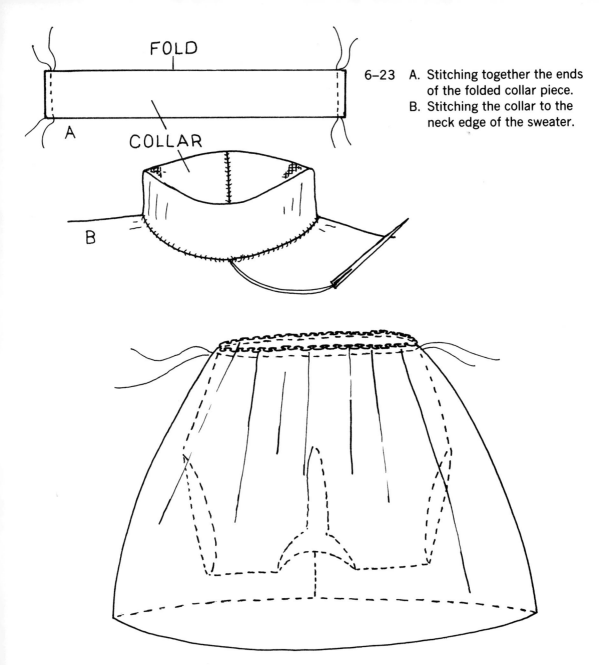

6-23 A. Stitching together the ends of the folded collar piece.
B. Stitching the collar to the neck edge of the sweater.

6-24 Stitching the skirt to the bodice.

HAT. To make the hat, stitch together the hat pieces from their base to the tip. Press the seam open. Using two rows of decorative stitching, cover each edge of the seam (fig. 6-25). Stitch the back edges of the hat together. Then, stitching close to the lower edge of the hat, run a line of decorative stitching around its base. Turn the hat right side out. Put it on Rumpelstiltskin's head with the two rows of decorative stitching in front. Flip up the front brim. You can stitch the hat to his head with a few concealed stitches, or leave it loose.

SHOES. Refer to figure 2-26 and stitch together one pair of shoe pieces. Stitch them together from the X marked at the upper back, around the heel and toe, to the dot marked on the upper front. Finish the shoe with a decorative stitch placed ¼ inch within the open edges. Assemble the second shoe.

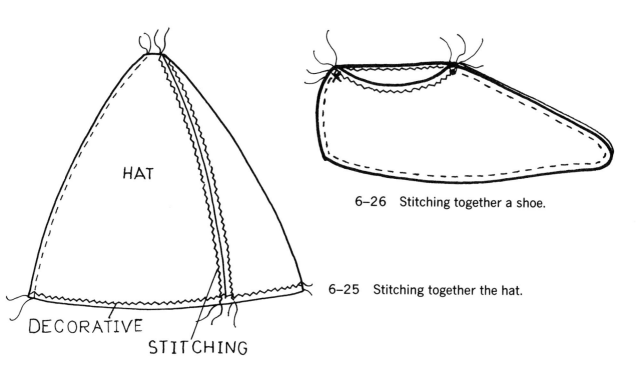

HAT

DECORATIVE

STITCHING

6-26 Stitching together a shoe.

6-25 Stitching together the hat.

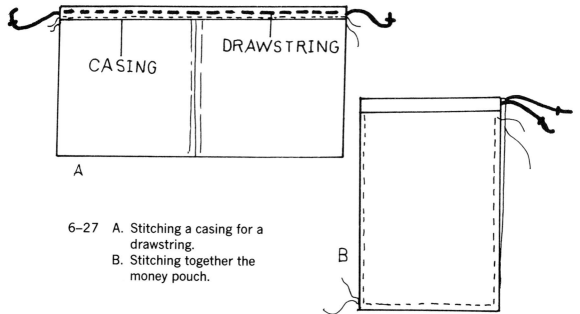

CASING

DRAWSTRING

A

6-27 A. Stitching a casing for a
drawstring.
B. Stitching together the
money pouch.

B

MONEY POUCH. Stitch together one long edge of the two pieces of the money pouch. Turn ½ inch of fabric along one short edge to the inside. Stitch close to the raw edge of the folded piece to form a casing for a drawstring (fig. 6-27A). Thread a 12-inch length of yarn or heavy twine through the casing, leaving the ends dangling an equal length from each side of the casing. Knot the ends. Stitch together the lower edge of the money pouch and the opposite long side (fig. 6-27B). End stitching at the lower edge of the casing so the strings remain free to draw up the fabric. Turn the money pouch right side out. Place a couple of pennies in the pouch. Draw up the string and tie it in a bow. Rumpelstiltskin can hold this pouch in his hand. The first composition project is complete.

CHAPTER 7
Project Two-The Snow Queen

7-1   The Snow Queen.

The snowflakes sprang to one side and the big sleigh stopped. The driver arose, cloak and cap smothered in snow. It was a tall and stately lady all shining white. It was the Snow Queen.

Hans Christian Andersen

The Snow Queen was designed with the old adage in mind, "simplicity is beauty." Her composition head displays only the barest suggestion of features, causing her ice-blue blown-glass eyes to appear startlingly bright. Her composition lower arms have simple spoon-shaped hands. Her composition lower legs feature molded, painted boots. The limbs are attached to a fabric body. Her head has a circumference of 10 inches. She is 15 inches tall. Her clothing consists of a white imitation fur cloak and cap. The cloak is decorated with a gray fur collar. She carries a gray muff. She wears a long-sleeved full-skirted print dress, a satin slip, and lacy pantalets.

The Head and Limbs

The head and limbs of the Snow Queen are constructed of composition applied over armatures. Read the section of Chapter Five that explains in detail building armatures and applying, drying, and finishing the surface of composition. A list of materials necessary to form the head and lower limbs of one doll follows.

7–2 The face of the Snow Queen.

Materials

One small round balloon
A section of cardboard cylinder measuring 1½
    inches with a diameter of 1½ inches
A sheet of newspaper
A piece of lightweight cardboard
Masking tape
A batch of flour and water paste
Paper strips
White glue
½ of composition Recipe I
Acrylic gesso, paints, and varnish

Blow up the balloon to a circumference of between 8 and 9 inches. Tape the knotted balloon to the cardboard cylinder (fig. 5-4A). Roll two strips of paper into tight cylinders that are narrower at one end (fig. 5-5). They should measure 3½ inches in length with a circumference of 2¾ inches at their widest point. Use tape to hold the rolls together. Using the pattern (fig. 7-3), cut two spoon shapes from lightweight cardboard. These are the hand armatures. Coat the tabs with glue and insert them into the narrow ends of the rolls. Roll two more paper cylinders measuring 3½ inches in length with a circumference of 4¼ inches at their widest point. Tape the rolls. Cut two boots (fig. 7-3) from lightweight cardboard and glue their tab ends into the narrow ends of these paper rolls.

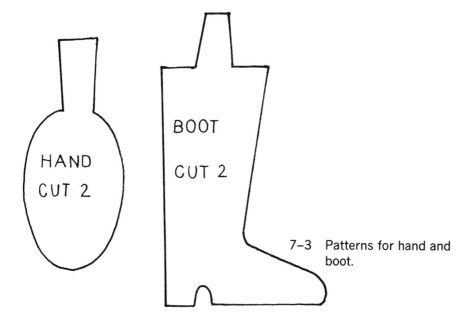

HAND

CUT 2

BOOT

CUT 2

7–3 Patterns for hand and boot.

Cover the armatures with strips of paper dipped in paste. After the first layer dries, apply a second layer. Build up areas, such as boots and portions of the head, before applying the final, third, layer of strips.

Coat each armature with diluted white glue and apply a thin layer of composition. When the composition is dry, apply the second layer. Model and smooth this final layer before it dries.

Rasp and sand the dry head and limbs to a desired degree of smoothness.

Because the Snow Queen has set-in eyes of blown glass, eye sockets must be cut in her face. Also, a circular piece is cut off the top of her head (fig. 7-5). Removing this piece allows room to reach inside the head and glue the eyes in position. After the eyes are set the piece is glued back on the head.

Refer to figure 7-5 and carefully saw a piece of composition the size of a silver dollar off the top of the doll's head. Save the piece.

Now, make two identical paper cutouts of the projected size and shape of the doll's eye sockets. The size and shape of the eyes have a great effect on the expression of the doll. You may wish to experiment with more than one paper cutout. A socket that is too large will show white around the iris and result in a startled expression. Sockets that are too narrow cover the iris and the doll appears sleepy. When you have decided, hold the paper piece in position on the head with straight pins (fig. 8-3). Lightly trace their outline with a pencil. Cut out the area within the pencil line using a sharply pointed tool such as a craft knife. Sand the inside edges of the sockets with a jeweler's file or a pencil wrapped with sandpaper. Place an eye in each socket to test for a correct fit. Cutting an accurate eye socket is tricky. You may wish to have more than one size of eye on hand to choose from.

Next, use an awl or drill and punch six equally spaced holes ¼ inch above the base of the head and encircling the neck (fig. 6-16).

Coat the surface of each of the composition pieces with two thin layers of gesso, allowing the first coat to dry before applying the second.

Mix a pale flesh color, using white, red, and a dab of yellow or blue acrylic paint. Coat the head, the piece removed from the top of the head, and the limbs with a smooth application of this paint.

Now, refer to fig. 7-2, which is a close-up of the Snow Queen's face. Using a pencil, lightly sketch her features on the head. Mix red and black to produce a reddish-brown acrylic paint. Paint delicate arching brows and two tiny dots for nostrils, and outline the mouth with this color. Soften the brown by mixing in a little flesh color. Use this to paint the inside of the eye sockets. Mix white and a little red to achieve a rosy pink. Paint small cheek patches. Gently rub a cotton cloth over this application of paint to blend the color into the face. Paint small dots of rosy pink on each side of the head to give the illusion of ears. The Snow Queen's boots are painted black. When the black paint is dry, decorate the outside of each boot with a curving green stem. Paint a simple pink flower, outlined with red, inside each curve of the stem (fig. 7-4).

Varnish all painted composition surfaces.

Setting the Eyes

The Snow Queen has a cool, Nordic expression accented by her ice-blue blown-glass eyes. Inserted eyes are more common than painted eyes, but glass is not the most common material. Wood, metal, celluloid, porcelain, buttons, cherry pits, tacks, beads, and jewels are a few of the materials that have served as the eyes of dolls. Glass eyes can be round or oval. Round eyes have

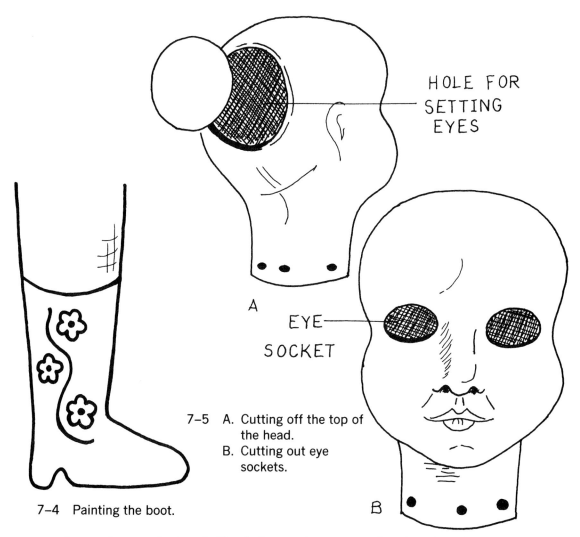

HOLE FOR SETTING EYES

EYE SOCKET

A

B

7-5 A. Cutting off the top of the head.
B. Cutting out eye sockets.

7-4 Painting the boot.

a stem and are easier to set. Blue is the most common color, though oval eyes can be purchased in brown or green. Brown and black were the predominate colors of eyes for early wooden dolls, but blue eyes have dominated the market ever since their introduction. Round or oval eyes can be ordered from suppliers of doll parts or specialists in glass eyes. Check the list of suppliers that follows the text.

Materials

One pair of blown-glass eyes (approximate diameter,
⁹⁄₁₆ inch)
Rubber cement
Composition or Sculpta Mold
White glue

To set the eyes, coat the insides of the eye sockets with rubber cement. This adhesive will hold the glass eyes temporarily in place while giving you time to correct errors in positioning. Place the eyes in the sockets. Position them carefully. To hold them permanently in place pack wet composition around the portion of the eye that is inside the head. The eyes should be pressed tightly into the sockets. If you do not have leftover composition and do not wish to make any, you can also use a commercial product called Sculpta Mold. It is available at most hobby and art-supply stores. Mix 1 tablespoon of Sculpta Mold with ½ tablespoon of water. The result is a sufficient amount of a pliable modeling compound for setting two eyes. Pack this material around the eyes. It dries hard within several minutes. An advantage to Sculpta Mold is that, if you make a mistake, you can moisten the material with a little water and it will fall apart, releasing the eyes. When the composition or Sculpta Mold is dry, you can clean rubber cement from the surface of the eyes with a toothpick.

After the eyes are set, glue the top of the head back in place with white glue.

The Wig

In keeping with the Snow Queen's northern European appearance, she has pale blond hair braided at the sides of her head. The wig is constructed of mohair yarn stitched to a fabric circle. For more information on this procedure, refer to the portion of Chapter Six subtitled "The Wig."

Materials

10 yards of mohair yarn
A scrap of fabric measuring 4 x 4 inches of the
      same color as the yarn
White glue
Thread to match the yarn

Cut a circle of fabric with a diameter of 4 inches. Stitch a line of basting stitches ¼ inch within the edge and around the circumference of this piece. Leave the ends of the thread dangling. Cut the yarn into 12-inch strands. Arrange half of the yarn over the surface of the fabric circle (fig. 6-3). Stitch the yarn to the circle. Arrange the remainder of the yarn over the circle, covering and at right angles to the first strands. Stitch this yarn in place. Draw up the basting stitches to form a fabric cup that fits over the crown of the Snow Queen's head. Coat the surface of the doll head (which is normally covered with hair) with a thin application of white glue (fig. 6-4). Press the wig in place. Hold the wig against the glue until it is dry by placing rubber bands around the head. When the glue is dry, plait the yarn into two braids.

The Body

The Snow Queen's head and limbs are attached to a fabric body. Leather or kid could be substituted for fabric. Her body is jointed with stitching at the shoulders and hips.

Materials

¼ yard of sturdy cotton or cotton-blend, flesh-
      colored fabric
Thread to match the fabric
White glue
Embroidery thread or sturdy string
¼ pound of polyester stuffing

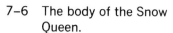
7-6　The body of the Snow
　　　Queen.

Using the pattern (fig. 7-7) as a guide, cut two fabric pieces. Transfer all markings to the right side of the fabric.

With right sides together, stitch the shoulder seams of the body from the notch at the neck to the end of the arms (fig. 7-8). Turn ¼ inch of the fabric along the base of each arm to the inside. Stitch close to the edge of these folded pieces, to form casings for drawstrings. Stitch the crotch seam. Press ¼ inch of fabric along the lower edge of each leg to the inside. Stitch, creating casings for drawstrings. Stitch the side seams. Do not stitch the ends of the casings closed (fig. 7-8). Turn the body right side out.

Thread a drawstring through each casing. A 7-inch length of sturdy string such as embroidery thread or nylon line will do. Leave sufficient string dangling from the ends of each casing to tie in a sturdy knot.

The composition limbs can now be attached to the fabric body. Begin by coating a ¼-inch strip at the base of one arm with white glue. Carefully slip the composition arm inside the torso (hand first), through the fabric arm, and out the opening. The broad base of the composition arm is wider than the fabric opening. Pull the arm through the fabric as far as it will go. Approximately 1 inch of the arm will remain inside the fabric. Position the arm with the thumb pointing upward. Draw up the string and gather the casing tightly around the arm. Tie the string in a knot. Add a drop of glue to the knot. Follow this procedure and attach the remaining arm and two legs to the fabric body.

Next, stuff the upper arms from the elbow to within 1 inch of the dotted stitching lines marked on the shoulders. Use small, pea-sized wads of stuffing. Round out the limbs but leave them soft and flexible. Machine stitch (twice) over the dotted lines marked where the arms join the shoulder. Stuff the legs to within 1 inch of the stitching lines marked at the hip. Machine stitch over these lines. Stuff the torso. The torso should be more firmly stuffed than the limbs. Leave sufficient room to insert the neck of the head ½ inch into the neck opening.

Turn ¼ inch of fabric around the neck edge of the torso to the inside. Cut six 6-inch strands of sturdy twine such as embroidery thread. Insert two lengths into each pair of holes in the neck of the head (fig. 6-16). Insert the neck into the torso opening. Stitch the ends of each strand of twine through the fabric of the body without removing them from the head. When all pieces have been drawn to the outside, tie each pair in a sturdy knot. Add a drop of glue to each knot. Stitch the shoulders of the torso together so it fits snugly around the neck.

The Snow Queen is assembled and can now be clothed.

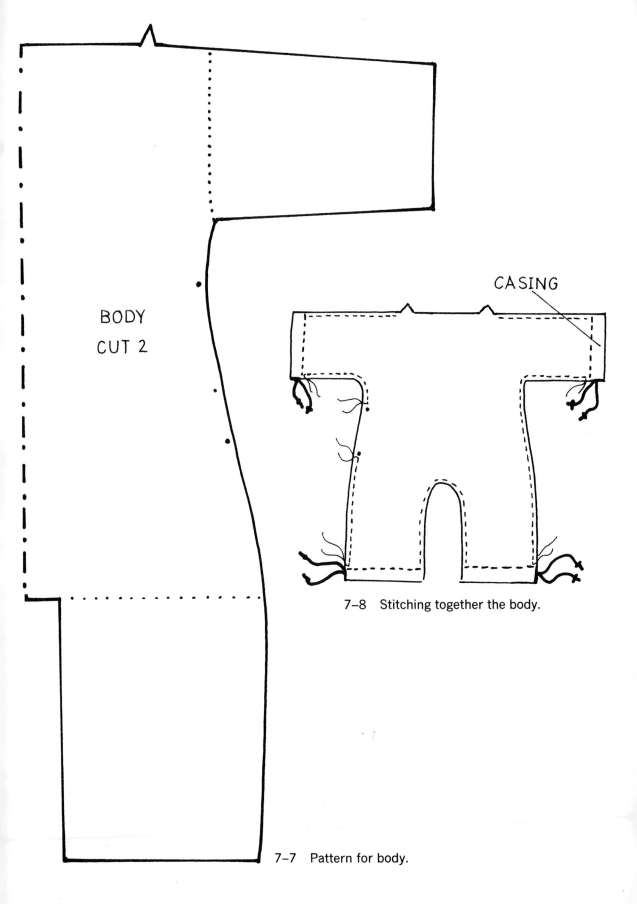

BODY

CUT 2

CASING

7-8 Stitching together the body.

7-7 Pattern for body.

The Clothing

The Snow Queen is dressed for the weather from which she takes her name. Her warm cloak is cut from white imitation fur and lined with white satin. The collar of the cloak is gray imitation fur and matches the muff suspended around her neck on a strand of black yarn. Her cap is white fake fur fabric with ribbon ties. The skirt and sleeves of her dress are made of a cotton-polyester-blend fabric and feature a tiny flower print. The bodice is navy-blue panne velvet. Her slip is satin and trimmed with lace. The pantalets are cotton, also laced trimmed. You can use these fabrics or substitute others. A list of necessary materials follows.

Materials

⅓ yard of imitation fur fabric for the cloak and cap
A 4 x 20-inch piece of another color of fur fabric for
    the collar and muff
⅓ yard of satin fabric for the lining of the cloak and
    the slip
¼ yard of fabric for the dress (sleeves and skirt)
A 6 x 8-inch scrap of fabric for the bodice
A 10 x 14-inch piece of cotton for the pantalets
1 yard of satin ribbon for the cloak and hat ties
A 20-inch strand of yarn for the muff strap
1 yard of ½-inch-wide gathered lace edging for the
    slip and pantalets
A 6-inch length of ¼-inch-wide elastic
4 tiny snap closures
Thread to match the fabrics

7–9 The Snow Queen's clothing.

Using the patterns (fig. 7-10, 7-11, 7-12) cut the correct number of pieces from the fabric you have chosen. Also, cut a rectangle of fabric measuring 12 x 18 inches for the cloak. Cut a rectangle measuring 12 x 18 inches for the cloak lining. Cut a rectangle measuring 4 x 11 inches for the cloak collar. Cut a rectangle measuring 9 x 21 inches for the skirt of the dress. Cut a rectangle measuring 8 x 18 inches for the skirt of the slip. Cut a rectangle measuring 3 x 5½ inches for the muff. Transfer all markings to the wrong side of the fabrics.

PANTALETS. Select the two pantalet pieces (fig 7-13). Align and stitch together one side from the waist edge to the base of the leg. Open out the piece. Turn ½ inch of fabric along the waist edge to the inside. Press. Stitch close to the raw edge of this folded piece forming a casing for elastic (fig. 6-21). Thread a 6-inch length of ¼-inch elastic through the casing. Stitch the elastic securely to both ends of the casing. Stitch the second side seam of the pantalets from the base of the leg to the waist edge, stitching the ends of the casing securely together. Turn and press ¼ inch of fabric along the base of each leg to the inside. Stitch these folded edges in place. Cut two 4½-inch lengths of gathered lace edging. Stitch a piece of lace to the base of each leg. Stitch the crotch seam, stitching together the ends of the lace as you do so. Turn the pantalets right side out and press.

SLIP. Stitch the slip's back bodice pieces to the front at the shoulder seams (fig. 7-14). Stitch the bodice side seams from the armholes to the waist. Hem the neck edge, the back opening edges, and the armhole openings.

Next, run a basting stitch ⅛ inch within and the length of one long edge of the rectangle of fabric cut for the slip skirt. Draw up the stitching, gathering the edge until it is the length of the waist edge of the bodice, overlapping the back edges by ½ inch (fig. 8-15). Align and pin the gathered edge of the skirt to the waist of the bodice (right sides together). Stitch the skirt to the bodice. Stitch the back edges of the skirt together from the base to within 1½ inches of the waist.

Hem the back opening edges of the skirt below the waist. Hem the lower edge of the skirt. Stitch two small snap closures to the neck and waist of the back of the slip. Turn the slip right side out and press it.

THE DRESS. To begin, stitch the bodice front to the two bodice back pieces at the shoulder seams (fig. 7-14). Turn ½ inch of fabric along each of the back opening edges to the inside. Press and then stitch these folded edges in place. Choose the rectangle of fabric that is to be the collar of the dress. Turn ¼ inch of fabric along one long edge to the inside (fig. 7-15). Press. Fold the piece in half so it is long and narrow. Press. Stitch the short ends of the piece together. Turn the collar right side out. Press. With right sides together, pin the unfolded edge of the collar to the neck edge of the dress. Baste. Stitch the collar to the dress. Press the seam upward toward the collar. By hand, stitch the folded edge of the collar over this seam.

The sleeves are next. Run a basting stitch ⅛ inch within the curved edge of each sleeve. Draw up this stitching so the sleeve is slightly gathered. Pin and then baste a sleeve to each armhole opening. Adjust the gathers so they are evenly distributed. Stitch the sleeves to the bodice.

Stitch the underarm seams of the bodice from the waist edge to the wrist ends of the sleeves (fig. 7-14). Hem the ends of the sleeves.

Attach the skirt of the dress to the bodice exactly as you attached the skirt of the slip to its bodice. Hem the back opening edges of the skirt to where they join the bodice. Hem the lower edge of the skirt.

Stitch two small snap closures to the neck and waist of the back opening edges. Press the finished dress.

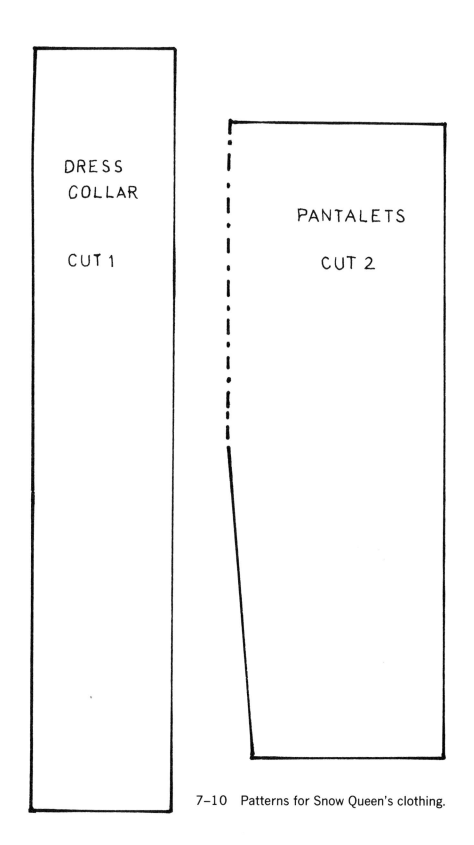

DRESS
COLLAR

CUT 1

PANTALETS

CUT 2

7–10   Patterns for Snow Queen's clothing.

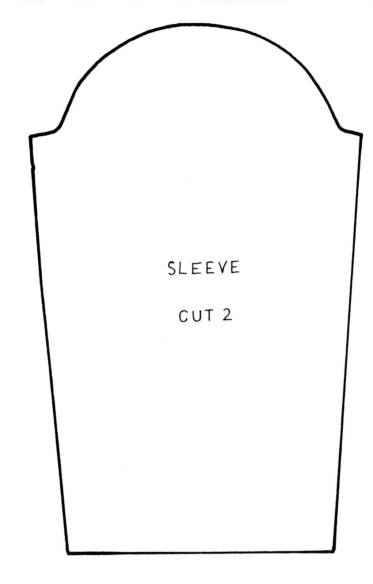

SLEEVE

CUT 2

7-11 Patterns for Snow Queen's clothing.

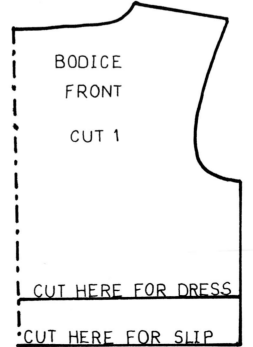

BODICE
FRONT

CUT 1

CUT HERE FOR DRESS

CUT HERE FOR SLIP

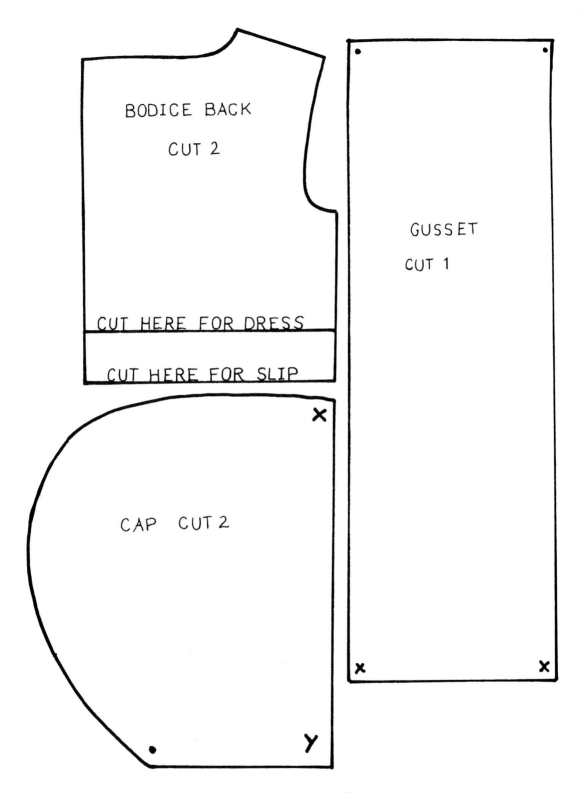

BODICE BACK

CUT 2

CUT HERE FOR DRESS

CUT HERE FOR SLIP

GUSSET

CUT 1

CAP CUT 2

×

× ×

Y

7–12   Patterns for Snow Queen's clothing.

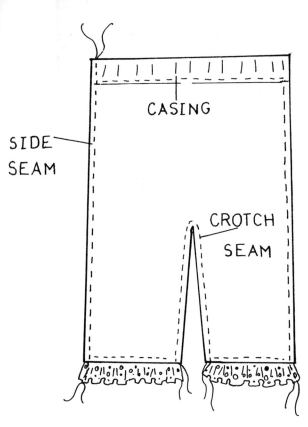

7-13 Stitching together the pantalets.

CLOAK. With right sides together, stitch the lining to the cloak. Place your line of stitching ¼ inch within the raw edges of the pieces and stitch around the entire perimeter. Leave a 2-inch opening through which to turn the cloak right side out. Turn and press, pressing ¼ inch of fabric along the opening edges to the inside. Then top-stitch ⅛ inch within the edges of the cloak, around the entire perimeter, stitching the open edges closed as you do so.

Run a line of basting ¼ inch within and the length of one long edge of the cloak. Draw up the basting and gather the cloak to a width of 10 inches. Stitch over the gathers to hold them permanently in place.

Press ¼ inch of fabric along one long edge of the collar of the inside (fig. 7-15). With right sides together, fold and press the piece in half the long way. Turn the collar right side out. Press. Align and baste the raw edge of the collar to the furry, gathered side of the cape (right sides together). Stitch the edges together. Press the seam toward the collar. Hand-stitch the folded edge of the collar over this seam. Press the cloak. Stitch a 10-inch length of ¼-inch satin ribbon to each front-opening edge of the cloak for ties.

CAP. Refer to figure 7-16 and stitch the gusset between the two cap pieces. Begin by aligning the dot on the gusset piece with the dot marked on one cap piece. Stitch the edges of the pair together from the dot to the X marked on both. Always ease the gusset to fit the cap, never the opposite. Stitch the second cap piece to the opposite side of the gusset. Hem all raw edges of the piece. Stitch a 6-inch length of ¼-inch-wide satin ribbon to the points marked with a Y on the inside of the cap. These are ties.

MUFF. Hem all raw edges of the rectangular piece that is to be the muff. Then roll this piece into a loose cylinder, overlapping the ends by 1 inch. Hand-stitch the overlap together (fig. 7-17). Last, attach the yarn strap by stitching one end of the strand of yarn through each end of the muff. Knot the yarn on the inside of the cylinder.

Dress the doll and she is completed.

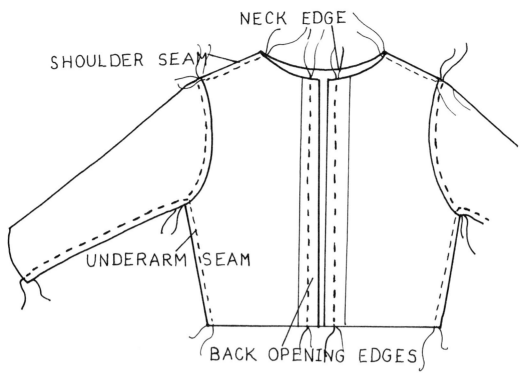

NECK EDGE

SHOULDER SEAM

UNDERARM SEAM

BACK OPENING EDGES

7–14   Stitching together the bodice of the dress.

FOLD

COLLAR

FOLD

7–15   Folding and stitching the narrow
ends of the collar.

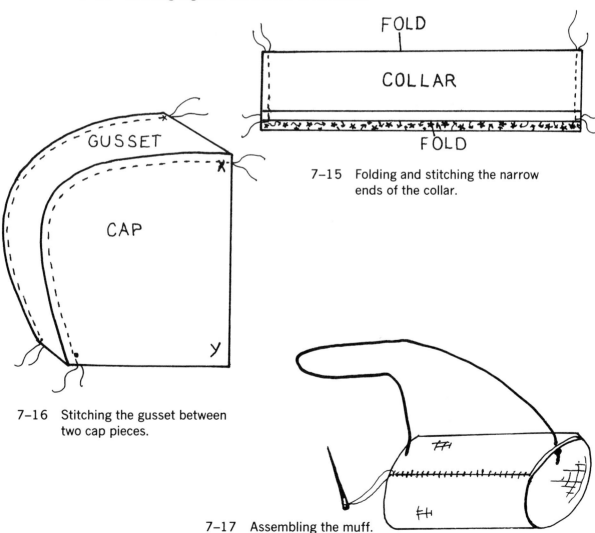

GUSSET

CAP

y

7–16   Stitching the gusset between
two cap pieces.

7–17   Assembling the muff.

CHAPTER 8
Project Three-Hansel and Gretel

8–1   Hansel and Gretel.

Gretel shook out her apron. She scattered the pearls and precious stones which she had gathered from the house of the wicked witch. The jewels were strewn on the floor in front of her father. Hansel added handful after handful out of his pockets. Their troubles had come to an end.

The Brothers Grimm

Hansel and Gretel are toddler dolls. They were modeled and dressed to represent young children. Their heads, torsos, and limbs are of composition that has been pressed into shape in plaster molds. They are 9 inches tall. Their heads have a circumference of 6 inches. The arms and legs of the pair are strung together with elastic cord and move in sockets cut in the torso. The dolls can stand, sit, and assume a variety of other positions. Hansel's clothes include white cotton underpants, a plaid flannel shirt, denim jeans, white ankle socks, and black felt shoes. Gretel is wearing white cotton underpants, a print dress, a lace-embellished print pinafore, white ankle socks, and brown felt shoes.

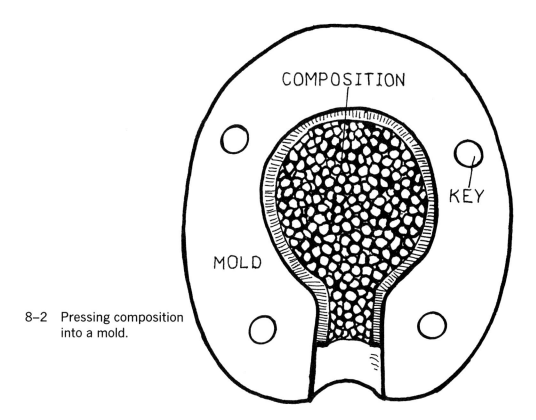

COMPOSITION

KEY

MOLD

8–2 Pressing composition
into a mold.

The Heads and Bodies

The shape and size of the heads, torsos, and limbs of Hansel and Gretel are identical. They are formed in the same plaster molds. The touches that make them individual are added during later steps. To begin the pair, read the section of Chapter Five that explains in detail the processes involved in casting composition. A list of materials necessary to make two dolls follows.

Materials

2 pounds of plastiline
12 cups of potter's plaster
Orange shellac
Vaseline
One batch of composition Recipe II
Acrylic gesso, paint, and varnish

Make plastiline models of the head, torso, and limbs of the projected doll (fig. 5-9). Be sure the pieces are in proportion to one another. Model rounded protrusions on the shoulder end of each arm and the top of each leg. These will fit into the sockets in the torso and serve as ball joints. Be sure the structure of the torso allows adequate room for the base of the limbs and the neck of the head. Do not hollow the torso. The arm, leg, and neck sockets will be cut out at a later point. To do so now would cause undercuts in the mold.

Divide the models with shims (fig. 5-10). Place each model in a nest of newspaper or fabric (fig. 5-11). Mix a batch of potter's plaster and water. One quart of water, to which has been added 6 cups of plaster, makes sufficient mixture to cast the models of the head, torso, and limbs. Pour the plaster over the models. When it has cooled, turn them over, placing the plaster-side down

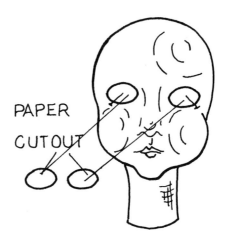

8–3 Pinning paper cutouts to a head as a guide to eye-socket placement.

PAPER CUTOUT

in the nest. Remove the shims. Make keys in the surface of the plaster. Coat the plaster with mold soap. Mix a second batch of plaster. Pour the second half of the molds. Allow the plaster to cool. Gently open the molds. Remove the plastiline models. Allow the molds to dry for two or three days.

Coat the casting surface and edges of the plaster molds with two thin, smooth applications of orange shellac. This will seal the surface of the plaster and allow it to release the composition from the mold. For added insurance, apply a thin even layer of vaseline over the orange shellac.

Press a uniform layer of composition into both sides of the mold (fig. 8-2). Clap the mold together as it is filled. Hold the molds closed with rubber bands until the composition has hardened.

Remove the pieces from the molds when they have dried sufficiently to hold their shape (at this point, you can refill the molds for the second doll). The pieces are still plastic. They will be fragile. Smooth the surface of the composition with your fingers or a flat, flexible tool such as a butter knife. Then use a template of small circles, a compass, or calipers and determine the size of the openings that the bases of the neck, arms, and legs will require. Lightly sketch a circle slightly larger (to allow for movement) than the base of each limb on the torso where the sockets will be (fig. 8-6). Carefully cut out the areas within the penciled outlines. Here again a sharp-pointed craft knife, such as an X-Acto knife, is the ideal tool. Use a jeweler's file or a pencil wrapped with sandpaper to smooth the edges and interior of these sockets.

Hansel and Gretel have set-in, oval, brown, blown-glass eyes. To make room to set the eyes, cut off the top of each doll's head. Remove a piece the size of a quarter (fig. 7-5). Save the pieces so they can be glued back on the heads after the eyes are set. Gretel's eyes are slightly larger than those of Hansel. I believe this accentuates her feminine appearance. Cut two almond-shaped paper cutouts the projected size and shape of each doll's eye sockets. Pin the paper cutouts to the respective doll's head, positioned where the eye sockets will be (fig. 8-3). Trace around the paper with a pencil. Remove the pins and pa-

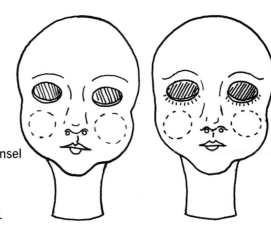

8–4 The features of Hansel and Gretel.

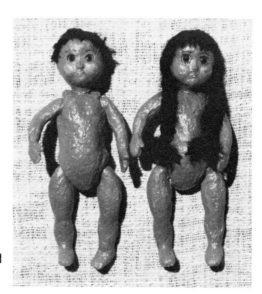

8–5 The bodies of Hansel and Gretel.

per. Cut out the eye sockets with a sharp-pointed craft knife. Drop the glass eyes into the sockets (Hansel's are 6/16 inch, Gretel's are 7/16 inch). If necessary, adjust the size and shape of the sockets for a correct fit. Sand the interior and edges of the sockets until they are smooth.

At this point you can add ears. Use leftover composition or mix a batch of composition Recipe III and model a set for each doll. Glue the ears to the sides of the heads with white glue.

Drill or punch a hole through the base of each limb (fig. 8-6). Elastic cord will be threaded through these holes when the body is assembled.

When the composition pieces are thoroughly dry, rasp and sand their surfaces to the desired degree of smoothness.

Next, coat all parts of each doll (including the top of the head) with two thin applications of acrylic gesso. Allow the first coat to dry before applying the second coat.

Hansel and Gretel (8-5) are painted a rich cocoa brown. Mix red, yellow, and blue acrylic paints to achieve a hearty brown. Add white and lighten the color. You will need approximately ¼ cup of paint to coat all the parts of the two dolls. Mix your paint in a small jam jar or a baby food jar that has a lid. Tightly seal the jar between work sessions so the paint will not dry out. In fact, it can be stored for several weeks. Paint all visible composition surfaces of the pieces of the dolls. When the paint is dry, check your work. Touch up any areas you may have missed.

Refer to figure 8-4. Use this drawing as a guide for sketching the features. Begin with Gretel. Paint her eyebrows black. Paint delicate black lashes below the eye socket. Paint the inside edges of the eye sockets dark brown. Mix white and red to achieve rosy pink. Paint the cheek patches with this mixture. Use a soft cotton cloth to run over the cheek color and blend it into the background. Paint the nostrils, the mouth, and a curved line inside each ear with this color. Outline the nostrils and the mouth with a deep red. Paint Hansel's eyebrows and eye sockets as you did Gretel's. Mix red, yellow, and white to create a pale red-orange color of paint. Paint the cheek patches, softening them with a cloth as you did Gretel's. Paint the lips, nostrils, and ear line of Hansel with this color. Outline the lips and nostrils with a dark, deep orange.

Varnish the dry painted surface with acrylic varnish. Set the pieces aside to dry.

Setting the Eyes

Refer to Chapter Seven, the subhead entitled "Setting the Eyes" for a detailed explanation of this procedure.

Materials

A pair of blown-glass eyes for each doll (⁵⁄₁₆ inch and
⁷⁄₁₆ inch)
Rubber cement
Composition or Sculpta Mold
White glue

Coat the inside of the eye sockets of one doll with rubber cement. Place the eyes in the sockets, positioning them carefully. When you are satisfied with the way they look, pack wet composition or Sculpta Mold around each eye. Be sure the eyes are pressed tightly into the sockets. Set the eyes in the head of the second doll following these same steps. When the composition or Sculpta Mold has hardened, remove any rubber cement from the surface of the eyes with a toothpick. Glue the tops of the heads back on the dolls with white glue.

Assembling the Bodies

A single strand of elastic cord is drawn through the arms and legs of each doll. The limbs are inserted into the sockets of the torso. The cord is drawn tight and knotted inside the neck opening. The elastic holds the limbs securely inside the torso, but is flexible enough to allow for a wide range of movement.

Materials

A 12-inch strand of elastic cord for each doll
One popsicle stick or pencil
White glue

Refer to figure 8-6. Thread elastic cord through the hole in the base of one arm. Leave a 2-inch segment of cord extending from the top of the arm. Draw the remainder of the cord out through the hole on the underside of the arm. Insert the base of the arm and the elastic into the arm socket. Draw the long end of the elastic through the torso and out the leg socket which is below the arm. Take care not to draw the elastic out of the arm. Thread the elastic through the hole in the base of the leg that fits in this socket. The cord should enter the hole on the topside of the leg and be drawn out the bottom hole. Insert the base of the leg and the cord into the socket. Draw the elastic across the base of the torso and out the leg socket directly opposite. Thread the elastic cord through the hole in the base of the leg that belongs in this socket. The cord should enter the hole on the lower side and be drawn out the top. Insert the cord and the base of the leg into the socket. Draw the cord up through the torso and out the last socket. Thread the elastic through the hole in the remaining

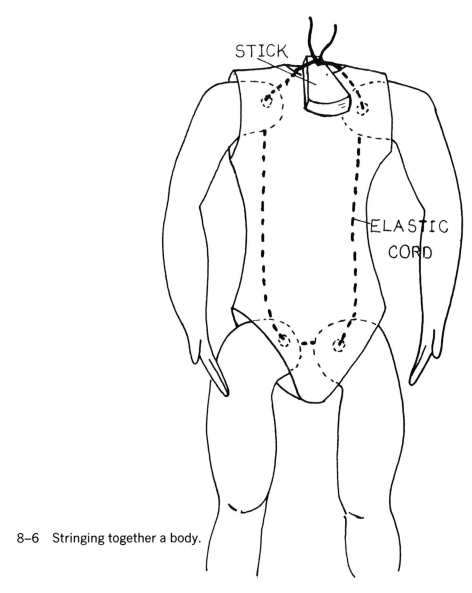

STICK

ELASTIC
CORD

8–6   Stringing together a body.

arm. The cord should enter the hole on the underside of the arm and exit out the topside. Insert the base of the arm and the elastic into the socket. Lay a popsicle stick across the neck opening (fig. 8-6). Draw the ends of the elastic cord that extend from the topside of the base of each arm out through the neck opening. One end of the cord should be on each side of the stick. Draw the cord tight, settling each limb securely in its respective socket. Knot the cord firmly over the stick. Withdraw the stick. The knot will drop back into the torso. The limbs should remain in their sockets but be mobile. If the thread is too loose, draw it tighter and retie it.

The heads of the dolls are fixed in one position. They are glued into the neck sockets. Coat the base of each neck with white glue. Place the necks in their sockets. Position the head before the glue dries.

The Wigs

Both toddler dolls have black mohair yarn hair. Hansel's is quite short and can be made from scraps of yarn that have been trimmed from the wigs of

8–7   Stitching pattern used for
Hansel's wig.

8–8   Hansel's clothing.

earlier dolls. Gretel's hair is long and braided. The yarn is stitched to a fabric circle that is glued to the doll's head. For more information about mohair yarn and the steps of this procedure, refer to the portion of Chapter Six subtitled "The Wig."

Materials

10 yards of mohair yarn for Gretel's hair
2 yards or scraps of mohair yarn for Hansel's hair
2 scraps of fabric measuring 2 x 2 inches
White glue
Thread to match the yarn

Cut a circle of fabric 2 inches in diameter for the wig of each doll. Stitch a line of basting stitches ¼ inch within the circumference of each. Leave the ends of the thread dangling.

To make Gretel's wig, cut 10 yards of yarn into 11-inch strands. Arrange half of the yarn across the surface of the fabric circle (fig. 6-3). Make three rows of stitching, transversing the fabric circle and attaching the yarn to it. Arrange the remainder of the yarn across the fabric, at right angles to the first. Stitch this yarn to the fabric. Coat Gretel's head with a thin application of white glue (fig. 6-4). Draw up the basting stitches that encircle the fabric patch, thus gathering the wig into a cup. Press the wig over the doll's head. Hold it in place with rubber bands until the glue dries.

A different procedure is used for Hansel's wig. His hair is short and should appear to sprout naturally from over the surface of his head. Cut the yarn for his wig into 1-inch and ½-inch strands. Arrange these strands (overlapping one another) on the fabric circle. Cover the surface. Stitch the yarn to the fabric with circular rows of stitching that decrease in size as you near the center of the wig (fig. 8-7). Coat Hansel's scalp with glue (fig. 6-4). Draw up the basting stitches. Press the cupped wig over the glue. Hold it in place with rubber bands until the glue dries.

Trim the yarn that falls over Gretel's face into bangs. Divide the remainder of her hair into two sections and braid it. Hold the braids in place with small rubber bands. Trim Hansel's hair. The strands will be different lengths. The yarn can be gently pushed into position with a soft hair brush.

The dolls are now ready to be clothed.

The Clothing

Hansel and Gretel are dressed in the style of country children. Hansel wears denim overalls, a plaid cotton flannel shirt, white cotton underpants, white knit ankle socks, and black felt shoes with embroidery-thread ties. Gretel's under-clothing, socks, and shoes are the same as Hansel's, except that her shoes are brown. She also wears a printed cotton dress and a printed cotton pinafore, the latter decorated with lace. Other fabrics can be substituted, but be sure to use a stretch fabric for the socks, or they will not fit. A list of materials necessary for their clothing follows.

Materials

⅛ yard of fabric for the overalls
⅛ yard of fabric for the shirt
⅛ yard of fabric for the dress
⅛ yard of fabric for the pinafore
A scrap of fabric measuring 5 x 5 inches for each
    pair of underpants
A scrap of stretchable fabric measuring 5 x 10
    inches for each pair of socks
A rectangle of felt measuring 4 x 5 inches for each
    pair of shoes
Two 8-inch strands of embroidery thread for each
    pair of shoes
Two 5-inch and one 1½-inch length of ¼-inch-wide
    elastic
A 22-inch length of ½-inch-wide gathered lace
    edging
8 tiny snap closures
Thread to match the fabrics

Use the patterns for the various articles of clothing (fig. 8-9, 8-10, 8-11) and cut the correct number of pieces from the fabrics you have chosen. Transfer all markings to the wrong side of the fabrics. Cut a rectangle of fabric measuring 3½ x 12 inches for the skirt of the dress. Cut another rectangle of fabric measuring 2½ x 12½ inches for the skirt of the pinafore. Cut two strips of fabric measuring ½ inch x 5 inches for overall straps.

UNDERPANTS. Both dolls wear the same size underpants. Follow these instructions and make a pair for each. Stitch together one side seam of one pair of underpant pieces from the base of the leg to the waist edge. Open out the piece. Turn ½ inch of fabric along the waist edge to the inside. Press this edge in place. Stitch close to the edge of the folded fabric, forming a casing for elastic (fig. 6-21). Thread a 5-inch length of elastic through the casing. Stitch the

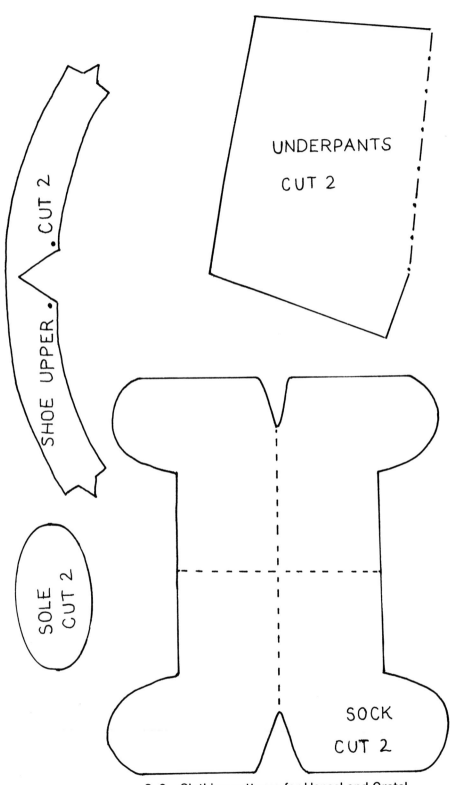

UNDERPANTS
CUT 2

SHOE UPPER · · CUT 2

SOLE CUT 2

SOCK

CUT 2

8-9   Clothing patterns for Hansel and Gretel.

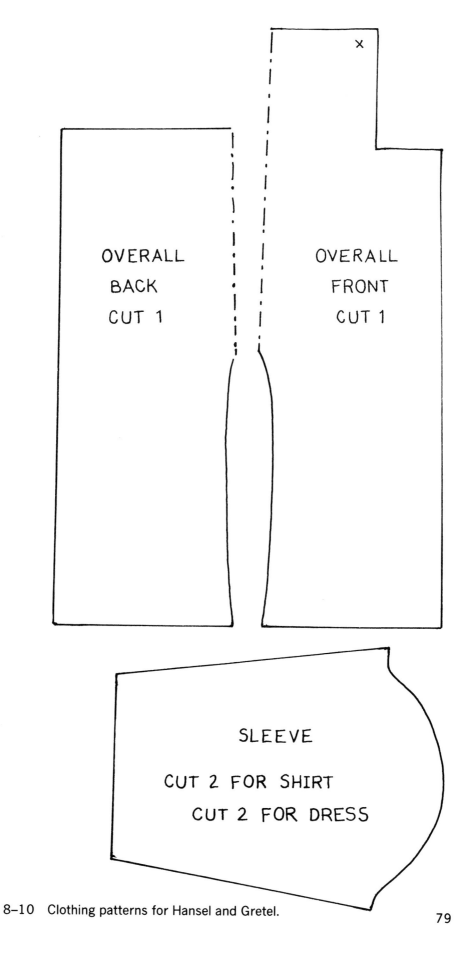

OVERALL
BACK
CUT 1

OVERALL
FRONT
CUT 1

×

SLEEVE

CUT 2 FOR SHIRT

CUT 2 FOR DRESS

8–10 Clothing patterns for Hansel and Gretel.

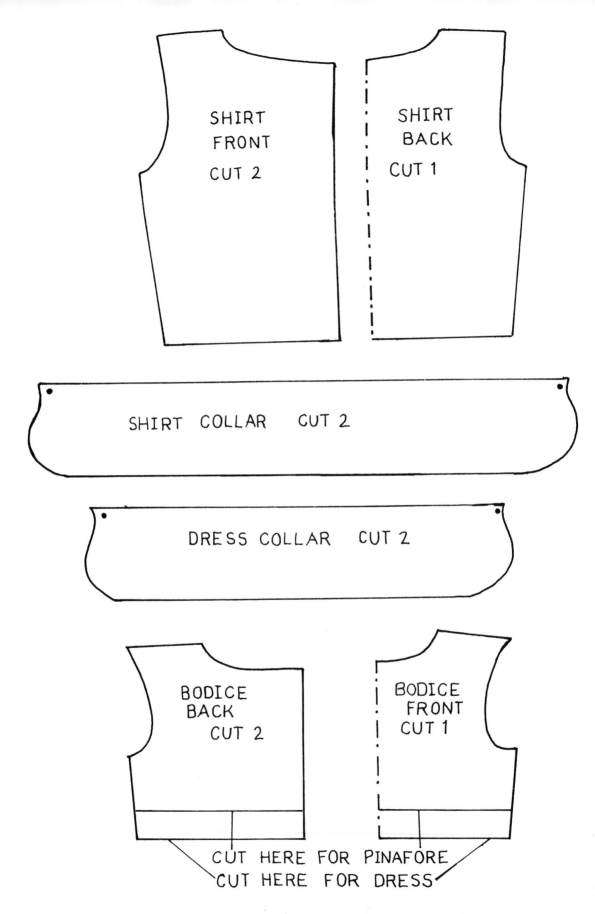

8-11 Clothing patterns for Hansel and Gretel.

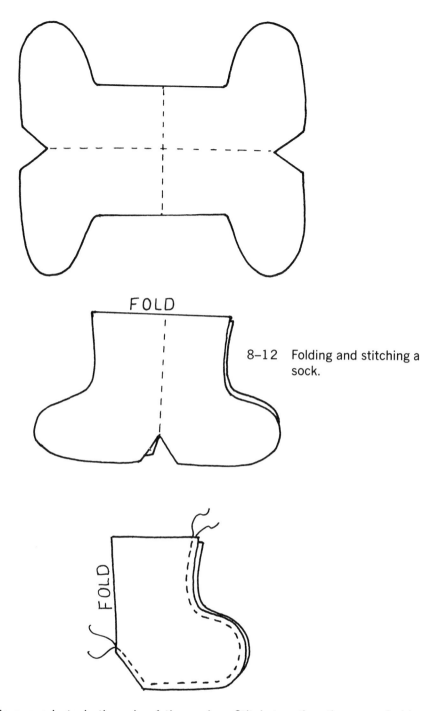

FOLD

FOLD

8-12   Folding and stitching a sock.

elastic securely to both ends of the casing. Stitch together the second side seam, stitching together the ends of the casing as you do so. Stitch the crotch seam. Hem the base of the legs. Press.

    SOCKS. Make a pair of socks for each doll. To begin, fold one sock piece along the fold line marked on the fabric (fig. 8-12). You now have a double layer of fabric. Next, fold the piece again so that the toes are together and you have four layers of fabric. Stitch from the top of the sock, down the front, around the toe, along the base of the foot, ending at the point where the fold begins. Turn the sock right side out. Turn ½ inch of fabric around the upper edge to the inside. Tack this edge to the seam with one or two stitches to hold it in place. Repeat this procedure and make the second sock.

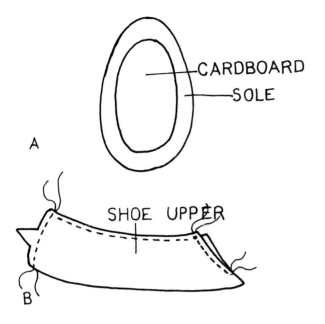

CARDBOARD

SOLE

A

SHOE UPPER

B

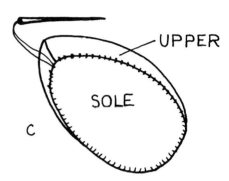

UPPER

C

SOLE

8–13 A. Gluing cardboard insert to felt sole.
B. Stitching heel and toe seam.
C. Stitching sole to upper.
D. Stitching laces to shoe.

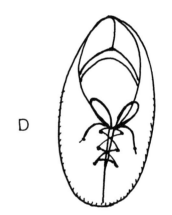

D

SHOES. The shoes are also the same for Hansel or Gretel. Follow the instructions and make a pair for each. Use the sole pattern for a guide and cut two soles from lightweight cardboard. Trim ⅛ inch from the perimeter of each of the cardboard pieces. Use an adhesive such as white glue, cloth glue, or liquid latex and glue a cardboard sole to the center of each felt sole, making sure you have a right and left sole. Figure 8-13 illustrates the steps of shoe construction.

Now, stitch together the toe of each shoe piece, aligning the dots marked on the pieces. Top-stitch close to the upper edge of each shoe piece. Then, fold one upper shoe piece so the notched ends of the piece are aligned. Stitch the ends together. Trim off the notch. Turn the piece right side out so the seams are on the inside. Repeat, stitching together the uppers of the remaining shoes. By hand, overcast-stitch a sole to the bottom side of each shoe upper. The cardboard insert should be on the inside of the shoe. To finish, stitch embroidery-thread laces (fig. 8-13D) to the shoes, drawing together ½ inch of the shoe toe beyond the seam.

OVERALLS. The overalls are gathered at the back waistband with elastic. To begin, turn ½ inch of fabric along the back waistband edge to the inside. Press this folded edge in place. Stitch close to the edge of the folded piece, forming a casing for the elastic (fig. 6-21). Thread a 1½-inch length of elastic through the casing, stitching it securely to both ends of the casing. Stitch the front of the overalls to the back along the side seams. Stitch from the base of the legs to the waist. Stitch the crotch seam from the inside base of one leg around to the base of the second leg. Hem the edges of the bib and the base of the legs. This can be done by hand or machine. A zigzag stitch and a contrasting color of thread add a nice decorative touch.

The straps are made of two strips of fabric that measure ¾ inch x 5 inches. Turn, press, and stitch ⅛ inch of fabric to the inside along each long edge of each strap. Fold the long way and press each strip in half, wrong sides together. Stitch the long edges of the folded pieces together. Narrowly hem the ends. Stitch a strip to the inside back of each side of the waistband. Stitch one-half of a snap closure to the front side of the opposite end of the straps. Stitch the opposite half of each snap to the X marked on the inside upper front of the bib. Press the overalls, creasing each leg, and they are finished.

THE SHIRT. Stitch the two front shirt pieces to the back piece along the shoulder seams. Hem the front opening edges of the shirt. To attach the collar, begin by pressing ¼ inch of fabric along the lower straight edge of one collar piece to the inside (fig. 8-14). Align the two collar pieces (with right sides together) and stitch together the curved edge between the dots. Turn the collar right side out and press. Align the right side of the unfolded edge of the collar with the right side of the neck edge of the shirt. Baste and then stitch the collar to the shirt. Press the seam toward the collar. Stitch the folded edge of the collar over the seam.

Next, insert the sleeves. Stitch a basting stitch ⅛ inch within the curved end of each sleeve. Draw up the stitching to slightly gather the sleeve. Align this edge with the edge of the armhole. Ease the sleeve to fit the armhole. Baste and then stitch the sleeve to the armhole. Attach the second sleeve. Stitch the underarm seams of the shirt from its base to the ends of the sleeves (7-14). Hem the sleeves and the base of the shirt. Stitch two snap closures to the front of the shirt. Place one snap just below the collar and the second halfway down the front of the shirt. Press the finished garment. Hansel's clothes are completed. Instructions for making Gretel's dress and pinafore follow.

THE DRESS. Begin by assembling the bodice pieces. Stitch the back bodice to the front along the shoulder seams (fig. 7-14). Hem the back opening edges. Press ¼ inch of the straight edge of one collar piece to the inside. With right sides together, align the two collar pieces. Stitch the curved edge of the pair together between the dots. Turn the collar right side out and press. Align the right side of the un-folded edge of the collar with the right side of the neck edge of the bodice (fig. 8-14). Stitch the collar to the bodice. Press the seam toward the collar. Stitch the folded edge of the collar over this seam.

Attach the sleeves to the bodice of the dress exactly as they were attached to the shirt. Stitch the underarm seams. Hem the sleeves.

To attach the skirt to the bodice, gather one long edge of the rectangle of fabric by basting ⅛ inch within one long edge and the length of the piece. Draw up the stitching. With right sides together, pin the gathered edge of the skirt to the waist of the bodice (fig. 8-15). The ends of the skirt overlap the back of the bodice by ¼ inch. Stitch the skirt to the bodice. Stitch together the back of the skirt from the base to 1 inch below the bodice (fig. 10-19). Hem the opening edges of the skirt below the bodice. Hem the base of the skirt. Stitch two snap closures to the back opening edges of the bodice. Place one at the waist and the second at the neck edge. Press the dress.

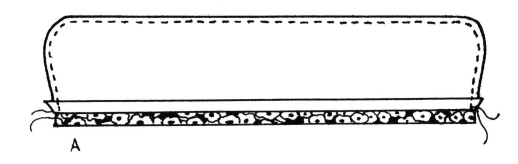

A

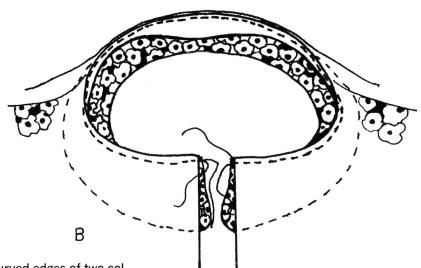

B

8–14 A. Stitching the curved edges of two col-
       lar pieces together.
    B. Stitching one edge of the collar to the
       neck edge.
    C. Stitching the folded edge of the collar
       over the seam.

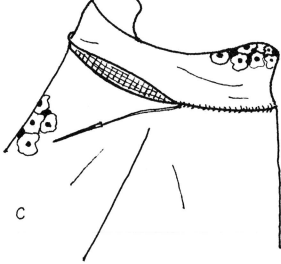

C

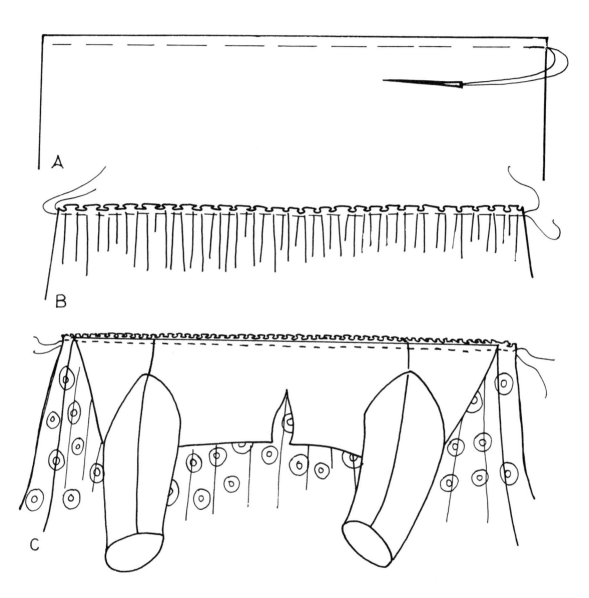

8–15 A. Basting close to one edge of the rec-
      tangular piece of skirt fabric.
      B. Drawing up the basting stitches,
      gathering the fabric.
      C. Stitching the skirt to the waist of the
      bodice.

THE PINAFORE. The pinafore is assembled in much the same way as the dress. Stitch the bodice front to the back pieces along the shoulder edges. Stitch the underarm seams. Hem the neck edge, the back opening edges, and the armhole edges. Attach the skirt to the bodice exactly as you attached the skirt to the dress bodice. Do not stitch the back edges of the pinafore skirt together. Hem these edges and hem the base of the pinafore. Stitch a 5-inch length of ½ inch-wide gathered lace edging around each armhole, hemming the ends of each piece. Stitch a 12-inch length of the same type of lace over the skirt hem to decorate the lower edge of the pinafore. Hem the ends of the lace. Stitch snap closures to the neck and waist of the back opening edges. Gretel's clothes are assembled.

Dress the pair, and Project Three—Hansel and Gretel—is completed.

SECTION II

CHAPTER 9
Bisque

9–1 Dry, unfired clay head.

Bisque dolls, coveted by collectors, became very popular during the late nineteenth century, though they were known to have been in demand as early as 1860 and were produced even before that date. The beautiful dolls made by the French dollmaker Jumeau were bisque. This type of doll almost always had a matte or nonglossy surface with occasional glossy decorations. The better grade of bisque doll was translucent. Hard- or soft-paste porcelain was the clay most often used. The early factory-produced bisque doll was pressed into the mold. However, as techniques improved, the clay was made liquid and was poured into the molds. An antique collector's definition of a bisque doll would be: a doll made of unglazed porcelain.

For the purposes of this book, bisque is defined as a ceramic clay piece that has been fired only once at a relatively low temperature. The surface of the clay is colored with bisque stains. These products air dry, eliminating the need for a second firing. A translucent sealer is brushed or sprayed over the layer of the color to protect and close the porous clay surface. A variety of types of clay that mature white or near-white when fired to cone 06 (1859° Fahrenheit) can be used. The low-firing temperature makes practical the use of a small, economical, electric test kiln. Bisque is an exciting and practical medium for the dollmaker to consider for hand-modeling original dolls. It can be a show-case for the techniques of the sculptor when modeling the doll parts, and can also put to use the painter's technique to enhance the doll's flesh and features.

THE CLAY

Clay is a natural material formed by the weathering action of time, which breaks feldspathic rocks into granules. Alumina and silica are the end products of centuries of decomposition. Natural clays are combinations of these materials, plus water and minerals.

Clays that remain where they were formed are called residual clay. Those that are moved some distance by wind or water and are deposited in a bed are called sedimentary clay. Residual clays are coarse, not plastic, and require extremely high temperatures to fire; but they fire beautifully white. Sedimentary clays are easier to work with but contain impurities and are much darker in color.

Ceramic clay bodies are blends of residual clay, sedimentary clay, and other substances that provide predictable results for each type of clay. Dollmakers must choose clays that suit their needs. All ceramic clays should be plastic and porous and they should come out of the kiln a predictable color and mature at a given temperature. The clay used by the makers of bisque dolls must fulfill even more specific qualifications: It must be a modeling clay; it should neither crumble nor collapse during the delicate job of building a doll; it must be sufficiently porous to dry rapidly without cracking; it must also withstand the heat of firing without cracking, or warping, or excessive shrinking. Specifically, for bisque dolls you should choose a modeling clay that matures at cone 06 and is naturally white or near-white with a porous surface after firing.

I will recommend two clays for bisque dollmaking, though there are others. I have extensively used S. H. Royal porcelain. It can be purchased from Sculpture House (the address is in the list of suppliers, in the back of the book). It is easy to handle. It fires pure white and opaque with an excellent staining surface at cone 06, but it also fires pure white and translucent at cones 2 through 9. There is a detailed discussion of the makeup of a porcelain clay body and its properties in Chapter Thirteen.

A second clay suited to the needs of the bisque dollmaker, and offered by most ceramic supliers, is white talc clay. It models easily. Though it is gray-white before firing, it fires intensely white with minimal shrinkage at cone 06. The surface is perfect for bisque-staining.

White talc clay is a low-fire white-clay body. Talc (natural hydrous magnesium silicate) is a flux. A flux is added to a clay body to bond the other components together and allow them to mature at a lower temperature than would be possible individually. An average white talc clay is composed of 30 percent china clay, 20 percent ball clay, and 50 percent talc. China clay is a residual clay that fires very white. Ball clay is an abnormally fine grained, plastic, sedimentary clay.

Modeling clay can be purchased moist and packed in plastic bags. It is de-aired, ensuring common properties throughout the mixture. The clay is ready to use and requires little wedging. It will remain in this condition if the bag is kept sealed, and can be stored for several months without further wetting. Modeling clay can also be purchased in a dry, powdered form. This clay flour

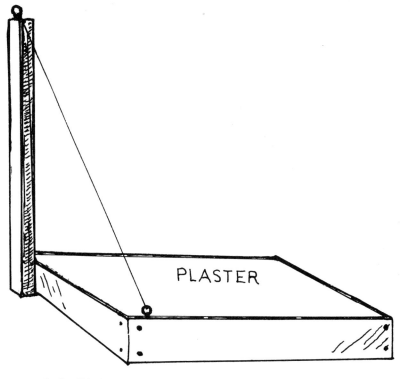

9-2 Wedging board.

PLASTER

is often less expensive and requires less storage space. One pint of water is added to 4 pounds of clay flour in a leakproof plastic bag. The bag is sealed and the mixture allowed to sit for several hours. Once kneaded, the clay is ready to use.

PREPARING CLAY

Before you begin to model clay it should be wedged. This process removes air pockets and renders the clay uniformly smooth and plastic. Wedging also mixes hard and soft portions of the clay body together, resulting in a mass of even consistency. And if the clay is too wet (won't hold a shape), wedging will remove some of the moisture. If the clay is too dry (shows cracks when bent double), spraying the surface of the clay mass with a light mist of water during the wedging process will add moisture.

An elementary and effective method of wedging clay is to knead it. Place a lump of clay on a flat work surface. Use both hands and lift the ends of the lump, simultaneously pressing the ends into the center of the lump. Then, using the heels of your hands, spread the lump into a thin pancake. Slightly rotate and then flip the pancake over. Squeeze the pancake into a lump, press the ends into the center, and repeat the entire process over and over. The pushing, pulling, and pressing encourage the flat clay particles to lie parallel to one another, increasing the workability of the clay.

For another method of wedging, cut the clay into sections and recombine it. A wedging board facilitates this procedure (fig. 9-2). It consists of a frame filled with plaster, with a taut wire attached. The clay is sliced into sections on the wire and recombined on the plaster surface. A list of materials necessary to make a primitive but functional wedging board follows.

Materials

A solid, shallow, wooden box measuring 18 inches
    square with a 4- to 6-inch depth
A 1 x 2 x 18-inch wooden post
Two screw eyes
One turnbuckle (optional)
A 30-inch length of 20-gauge rustproof wire
Plaster

To begin, fasten the wooden post to one side of one corner of the wooden box. Line the interior of the box with plastic to make it leakproof. Or, place the box on a glass or plastic work surface and build retaining walls of plastiline or water clay around its exterior. Mix a batch of plaster (following the instruction in Chapter Five). Fill the box with plaster.

If you have any leftover plaster, pour it into disposable aluminum frozen-food containers, the interiors of which have been coated with cooking oil. These rectangular and round plaster forms are called bats. Bats have many functions. For example, they can be used to support clay work in progress or aid in drying the model. When the bats are cool and hard, they should be removed from their containers and stored.

To proceed with the wedging board, allow the plaster in the wooden box to cool and harden. Then attach a screw eye to the top of the wooden post. Attach a second screw eye, directly opposite the first, to the frame of the box. Attach the wire and optional turnbuckle between the two screw eyes. Make the wire taut.

Use the board to wedge the clay following this basic procedure. Draw the lump of clay up from underneath, against the wire, slicing it into two equal sections. Throw one-half of the clay aggressively against the plaster surface of the wedging board. Slam the second clay piece on top of the first. Pick up the combined lump and forcefully throw it onto the plaster. Do this several times. Then, again, slice the clay, repeating the entire process over and over until the consistency of the clay is correctly plastic.

MODELING

Wedged clay is prepared for modeling. Display the preliminary sketches (pencil or clay) of the proposed doll near your work area. A plastic turntable or a more professional modeling stand is a handy additional aid but not absolutely necessary. However, do build your piece upon a surface that can be easily turned without touching the model. A plaster bat, dinner plate, or smooth board will suffice.

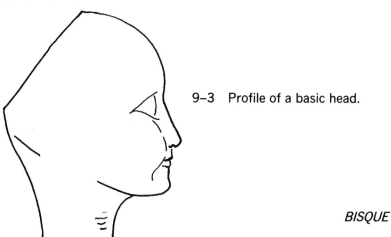

9–3   Profile of a basic head.

Begin building the head by squeezing the basic shapes from a lump of clay. Keep in mind that clay shrinks as it dries and still more when it is fired. Plan on 16- to 20-percent shrinkage. Construct an egg shape with a cylindrical neck that extends at an angle from the underside and broadens into a shoulder-shaped block (figs. 9-3, 9-4). The block can be developed into a shoulder plate, or the head can be cut off at the base of the neck, depending on whether you are modeling a shoulder-head doll or a swivel-head doll. The block provides a sound foundation during this early stage of modeling.

For now, avoid any attempts at smoothing the surface or working in minute detail. Build a basic facial structure, beginning with cheeks, chin, forehead, and the back of the head. As these develop, proceed to the nose, lips, ears, and eyes. A compass or calipers are helpful to measure parts of the face—such as the eyes—that should remain equal in size. From time to time, observe your work in a different light or hold it up to a mirror. Structural errors are sometimes more noticeable under these circumstances.

Take care when adding clay to the surface of a piece. Air pockets can be trapped beneath additions, causing them to blow off during the firing cycle. Be sure added clay has the same moisture content as the basic structure. Blend additions well into the surface.

Use the carving away of clay as well as adding it as a technique to develop shape and form.

Keep your piece moist as you work. A sprayer (like the kind used to mist house plants) should be kept handy. Fill it with water. Lightly mist the clay surface as it becomes dry. Store unfinished pieces in an airtight plastic bag between work sessions.

Figures 5-8 and 11-3 show some ceramic modeling tools that can be helpful. Items found in the household can also be put into service. A kitchen knife, a toothpick, an embroidery needle, a wooden dowel stick, or a pencil can be used to push clay around, remove clay, or texture its surface.

When you are satisfied with the structure and shape of your clay head, add detail and smooth the surface. If you plan a swivel-head doll, cut the base of the neck off at the shoulder block. A doll that is to have set-in eyes should have the top of the head sliced off (fig. 7-5A). Smooth the edges.

Follow these same general instructions to model torsos, arms, and legs. Specific information on modeling an entire bisque body can be found in Chapter Eleven.

Never wash clay down drains; like plaster, it will create a plug.

DRYING

Clay is pliable because it contains water, called water of plasticity. As the clay dries, this water evaporates and the tiny granules making up the clay move closer together. In other words, the clay shrinks. If portions of the piece dry more rapidly than others, either the clay shrinks unevenly and cracks, or warping occurs. Ceramic clay also contains atmospheric water and chemically combined water, which are present even in bone-dry clay. This water is driven off in the kiln when the piece is fired.

Two precautions can be taken to protect the head or body pieces of a doll from damage during drying at room temperature. First, the drying time of the exposed upper surface (which dries fastest) can be slowed by covering it with a piece of damp, lightweight fabric (such as cotton sheeting). Spray the cloth

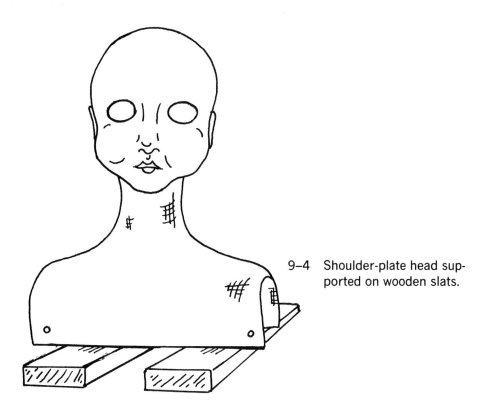

9–4 Shoulder-plate head supported on wooden slats.

9–5 Loop-ended modeling tool.

from time to time with a light mist of water to keep it moist. The fabric can be removed for gradually extended periods of time as drying progresses. Second, expose the underside of the clay piece to the movement of air (fig. 9-4) by raising it above the work surface. Place the model on two separated wooden supports (2 x 2 x 6-inch wooden slats are suitable).

Clay becomes hard by degrees. The first stage of drying is termed "leather-hard." The clay is firm, no longer plastic, but still damp. At this point the surface of the clay can be carved but not modeled. Now is the time to hollow out your piece. A doll model should have walls of uniform thickness. If not, it heats unequally during firing and the piece may crack. Walls should be no thicker than ½ inch for a small doll to ¾ inch for a larger head. Use a tool with a wire loop end (fig. 9-5) and scoop out the clay through the opening in the base of the neck, shoulder plate, or back of the head. Also hollow out torsos and limbs. When finished, pieces should be hollow, with walls generally of uniform thickness.

The leather-hard stage is also the time to cut out areas that require the same treatment—for example, eye sockets or torso sockets. Also, make holes for attaching shoulder plates to fabric bodies, or threading elastic through the base of limbs.

Again, place the clay piece on wooden slats and cover it with damp sheeting to control the drying process. The doll is now allowed to become "bone dry." When the clay has reached this degree of dryness, all water of plasticity will have evaporated. This will take ten days to two weeks, depending on the size of the piece. The final stage of drying takes place in the kiln.

If further smoothness is desired the bone-dry piece can be sanded with a piece of nylon stocking or a fine grit scrubber. Wear a face mask during this procedure to avoid inhaling the fine dust that rises from the surface of the clay.

MENDING

If your clay piece breaks during drying, don't lose heart. Pieces of clay can be joined to one another if the moisture content in the parts to be connected is equal or made equal. First, roughly texture the edges to be joined. Coat the edges with slurry. Slurry is clay dissolved in enough water so it has the consistency of heavy cream. A few drops of vinegar can be added to the slurry. Acetic acid is said to form a better bond between the edges by increasing the attraction of the clay particles for one another. Press the slurry-coated edges firmly together. Blend the inside and outside surface of the clay over the joint, concealing it completely. At this point, the piece can continue to dry normally unless the moisture content of the pair is unequal. In this instance, spray the entire surface of the piece, including the joined edges, with a light misting of water. Place the model in a sealed plastic bag. Allow it to sit undisturbed overnight. Capillary action will equalize the moisture throughout the piece. Then, dry as usual.

THE KILN

Many dollmakers never own a kiln. In most areas you can find ceramic shops that will fire work for local ceramicists. The shop managers rent kiln time and take responsibility for the entire firing process. The cost depends on the maturing temperature of the clay to be fired. For instance, bisque fired to cone 06 (1859° Fahrenheit) will cost less than porcelain fired to cone 6 (2246° Fahrenheit). Sometimes costs can be cut by sharing a kiln load with other people who have compatible pieces to fire.

I recommend that you read the segment on firing even if you plan to have someone else fire your work. There are special considerations that should be given to hand-modeled pieces which are not necessary when firing slip-cast greenware. Acquaint the person who is to fire your work with these individualities.

For those of you who plan to purchase a kiln, a brief discussion of what the dollmaker requires follows.

Select a kiln that is capable of reaching the maturing temperature of the highest-fire clay you plan to us. Most dollmakers eventually make plaster molds and cast dolls of porcelain slip. Porcelain requires firing to 2246° Fahrenheit to acquire the true luster and translucency of the clay. A dollmaker's kiln should be capable of reaching this temperature in a reasonable amount of time.

Next, it is absolutely necessary that the firing chamber of the dollmaker's kiln have equally distributed heat. If sections of the kiln reach different temperatures, the clay piece will be subjected to unequal heat, and this can cause warping. Choose a kiln with heating elements in all four sides of the firing chamber to help assure even heat distribution. To check a firing chamber, place pyrometric cones in a variety of locations throughout the interior of

9-6   Electric test kiln.

the kiln. Fire the kiln to the temperature at which the cones bend. Check to see if the cones responded uniformly.

Also, select a kiln in keeping with the amount of work you plan to produce and the space you have at your disposal. A large kiln is expensive to purchase, expensive to run, and requires a large permanent area in which to be set up. If you are an individual dollmaker, planning to fire only a few pieces a week, a small kiln is most practical.

Another consideration is the source of power. Choose a kiln that uses a convenient fuel. Only a dollmaker with a source of natural gas, a large studio, and a chimney can afford to consider a gas-fired kiln. Small portable electric kilns are the most practical for the average dollmaker.

Last, because porcelain, bisque, and china painting are easily contaminated by impurities inside the kiln during the firing cycle, choose a kiln that can be kept clean. A kiln without hard-to-reach crooks and crannies will be easier to maintain.

There is an inexpensive test kiln on the market that meets the requirements of the beginning dollmaker, or anyone who does not fire a large volume of work (fig. 9-6). Its cost, including shipping, is well under one hundred dollars. A ceramic supply shop that offers these kilns for sale is mentioned in the list of suppliers. The kiln runs on 110–115 volts of household current and draws 13 amps. The interior of the firing chamber is 6 x 6 x 4½ inches. The size can be increased by the addition of a 2½-inch blank ring or a 4½-inch element ring (purchased separately from the basic kiln). The kiln fires to cone 018 in fifteen minutes and cone 6 in one hour. Additional equipment such as a time clock, pyrometer, and infinite control can also be purchased from the supplier. The heating element is tightly coiled nichrome wire set in grooves in the firebrick. It can be easily replaced. All the dolls featured in this book were fired in this kind of kiln. I do, however, suggest that the base of the kiln be placed on a layer of firebrick when the kiln is being fired. This precaution will safeguard against any heat that may escape around the bottom of the kiln. Four standard 2½ x 4 x 9-inch firebricks can be purchased at any masonry supply store, and they serve this purpose adequately.

To assure consistent good results, keep your kiln clean. It is a good idea to gently vacuum the cooled interior of the firing chamber, the heating elements, and their grooves after each firing. A household vacuum with a crack-cleaning or soft brush attachment can be used for this job.

Also, heating elements wear out. Wire elements calcify. They acquire a coating and become inflexible, limiting the amount of heat they produce. Eventually they break and do not heat at all. You can test your elements by turning on the kiln and after two minutes quickly touching them with the tip of a tightly rolled paper towel. If the towel begins to smoke, the element is working. This procedure can be hazardous, so take precautions. Replace heating elements that are not working properly. Ceramic suppliers list elements for standard kilns in their catalogs.

FIRING

Firing turns water-base clay rocklike and hard. This physical change is called "maturation." Ceramic clays mature at specific temperatures depending on the makeup of the body. Underfired clay is chalklike, and overfired clay can melt into a formless mass. So, before you fire your doll parts, you must be able to measure the temperature inside the firing chamber. Electric kilns can be equipped with pyrometers. A pyrometer gives an exact reading of the temperature inside the kiln. If you do not have a pyrometer or would like an additional safeguard, you can use pyrometric cones.

Pyrometric cones, composed of clay and fluxes, are slender three-sided pyramids that soften and bend at specific temperatures, signaling when the firing chamber of the kiln has attained a specific degree of heat. Small cones, used in small kilns, are about 1¼ inches tall. Large cones are 2½ inches tall. Large cones bend at slightly lower temperatures than small cones. The temperatures I give are those at which small cones bend. Each cone is numbered. The numbers are standard and indicate the temperature at which the cone bends. Cones numbered 022 bend at the lowest temperature (1165° Fahrenheit). Cone numbers decrease and bending temperatures increase through cone 01 (2152° Fahrenheit). The next cone number on the scale is cone 1 (2154° Fahrenheit) and on up to cone 12 (2471° Fahrenheit). Pyrometric cones have been used so long and dependably that ceramacists and sculptors always refer to the firing temperatures of their clay and glazes by cone numbers and not degrees Fahrenheit.

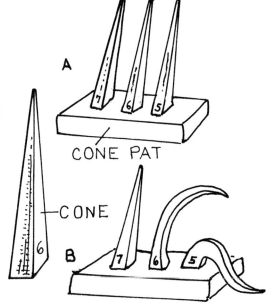

9–7 A. Pyrometric cones in a cone pat.
      B. Appearance of cones when kiln should be turned off.

To prepare the kiln for firing, three cones in a cone pat are placed inside the firing chamber. Locate the cone pat where it will be visible through the peephole of the kiln. A cone pat is a lump of grogged clay with triangular indentations to hold the base of the cones (cone pats can be purchased from ceramic suppliers or you can make your own, but be sure they are bone dry before use). Position the cones slanting to the right (fig. 9-7A). If they are positioned vertically, they will slump instead of bending. The center cone should bend at the temperature at which the clay being fired matures, or the temperature at which you plan to turn off the kiln. The two remaining cones are controls. The cone to the right should measure one temperature (on the cone scale) lower than the center cone. When it bends you know the kiln will soon reach the projected firing temperature. The third cone measures the next temperature higher than you plan to fire. This cone should not bend. Turn the kiln off when the middle cone has begun to noticeably bend. As an example, a cone pat for firing a bisque doll should contain (*from right to left*) cone 05, cone 06, and cone 07.

Place a ½-inch layer of dry hydrated alumina on the shelves before putting the clay pieces in the kiln. Alumina is a highly heat-resistant ingredient of clay. Placed on kiln shelves it provides excellent footing for the models during firing. It helps prevent contamination and controls warping. It can be reused.

Arranging pieces in the kiln prior to firing is called "stacking." A variety of shapes and sizes of hard fireclay supports (called kiln furniture) can be purchased to aid this arrangement. In general, doll parts should be placed on shelves with ½- to 1-inch legs. This allows heat to circulate beneath the clay. Never place doll parts on the floor of the kiln. Be sure pieces do not touch one another. Allow an inch or two between them. Doll heads should be placed upside down, facing inward.

The first portion of the firing cycle is called the "water smoking period." This is when any atmospheric water (which is present even in bone-dry clay) escapes. If you are using a kiln that does not have a flue, leave the kiln door cracked and the peephole open for the first half hour. Then partially close the door and the peephole and wait another half hour. At the end of this period close the kiln. Cracking the door allows the atmospheric water to escape without damaging the pieces in the kiln.

The next change that occurs is the disappearance of chemically combined water. This water is part of the molecular structure of the clay. Just before the clay becomes red hot complete dehydration occurs.

Next, a critical physical change occurs and silica in the clay expands. Finally, vitrification takes place and the clay matures. At this point, the alumina and silica interlock and combine with the fluxes. The clay particles fuse, becoming dense, hard, and glassified. The kiln is shut down.

Do not open the kiln. It must cool slowly. The cooling process should take longer than it took to heat up the kiln. Allow six hours for a small electric test kiln to cool, and longer for larger kilns. The kiln can be opened when it has dropped to 200° Fahrenheit. If the kiln is opened too soon, the doll parts may crack. Be patient. If a piece is too hot to handle, it is too hot to be removed from the kiln.

BISQUE-STAINING THE SURFACE

The cooled, fired doll parts can be polished with extrafine sandpaper or fine grit scrubbers to the desired degree of smoothness. A tiny jeweler's file

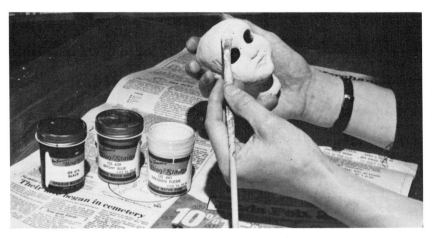

9–8   Bisque-staining a doll head.

wrapped with extrafine sandpaper can be used to sand crevices. Do not use coarse products. They will scratch the surface. Be sure the clay piece is clean, dry, dust- and oil-free before applying bisque stain.

Bisque stains are paints formulated to adhere to the surface of ceramic ware. They can be purchased premixed in fluid form, in two-ounce jars. A broad array of colors is available and they can be intermixed to produce a great many tints and shades. The colors are water soluble when wet. Once bisque stain has been applied to a clay piece it dries and sets naturally. Do not fire the piece. Opaque colors are best for staining the surface of the doll parts, but translucent colors can be used for special effects. The first coat of color should be scrubbed into the soft bisque (cone 06) surface with a bristle brush for solid-color coverage. To begin, acquire a bright blue, bright yellow, bright red, black, white, and perhaps a flesh color of bisque stain. Any other colors you may need can be mixed. More specific information on mixing colors and painting flesh and features can be found in the chapters that present bisque projects.

When you first open a jar of stain, use the color on the lid. Otherwise, it will dry, chip off, and fall into the paint in the jar. It will not redissolve, and it may spoil the surface you are painting. Be sure to stir the colors thoroughly. Wipe clean the insides of the lids and the rims of the jars before closing. Store the jars tightly closed. Opaque colors can be thinned with water. The colors dry hard and insoluble. Wet stain can be removed from hands, brushes, and other surfaces with soap and water. Dried stain must be removed with a solvent purchasable from the supplier of the stain.

You will need brushes. The same brushes that I recommend for use with acrylics in Chapter Five I also recommend for use with bisque stains. Use the information provided in Chapter Five when choosing sizes and shapes of brushes. Also, follow the same instructions for preparing brushes for use, checking a point, and cleaning brushes. One set of brushes, carefully cared for, can be used for both acrylic paints and bisque stains.

The stained surface of the doll can and should be given some additional protection by coating it with a ceramic sealer. The sealer dries quickly, clear, and hard. Sealer can be purchased in gloss, matte, or flat matte form. Stir well before using. Apply two thin coats with a soft brush.

The three chapters that follow contain specific instructions for modeling, firing, staining, and clothing four bisque dolls.

CHAPTER 10
Project Four-The Beauty and the Beast

10–1   The Beauty.

Turning to ask the Beast what it could all mean, Beauty found he had disappeared, and in his place stood a handsome prince!

Madame De Villeneuve

The Beauty and the Beast are modeled of S. H. Royal porcelain (white talc clay can be substituted) and bisque-fired to cone 06. The surfaces of the dolls are finished with bisque stain that has been coated with sealer. They have shoulder-plate heads. The lower limbs of Beauty and the lower arms of the Beast are also bisque. The doll parts are attached to fabric bodies.

The Beast is a multiface doll. One face represents the Beast, the other, that of the handsome Prince. Dollmakers in their never-ending search for uniqueness have produced two-in-one-dolls (dolls with a second head concealed under their skirts in place of legs) and multihead dolls as well as multiface dolls.

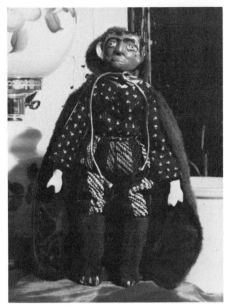

10-2   The Beast.   10-3   The Prince.

They have made the popular two-face doll, utilizing all common dollmaking materials. Documentation exists describing dolls with as many as five faces. A U.S. patent for a four-faced doll was obtained in 1866.

The hood of the Beast's long fur cloak hides one face when the other is in use. Besides the cloak, he wears pantaloons, a long-sleeved, V-necked shirt, and cotton underpants. In keeping with his dual personality, his clothing displays a different set of fabrics and colors on each side. His boots, made of imitation brown fur fabric, are stitched permanently to the fabric of the upper leg. Claws are embroidered on the back side of the boots to give the illusion that his legs end in paws. The Beast/Prince is 14 inches tall. His head has a circumference of 8 inches.

The Beauty wears a brocade gown, satin slip, lacy pantalets, and black felt boots and spats. Beauty's height is 12½ inches. The circumference of her head is 7 inches.

Modeling

Before beginning modeling the dolls, thoroughly acquaint yourself with the information presented in Chapter Nine. Remember to take into consideration the approximate 20-percent shrinkage of the clay during drying and firing. Model a head with a 10-inch circumference so the finished doll will have a head circumference of 8 inches. A list of materials necessary to make the bisque portions of one girl doll and one multiface doll follows.

Materials

A lump of wedged modeling clay that matures white
     or near-white at cone 06 to model the shoulder-
     plate head, lower arms, and lower legs of Beauty
     (approximately one pound of clay)

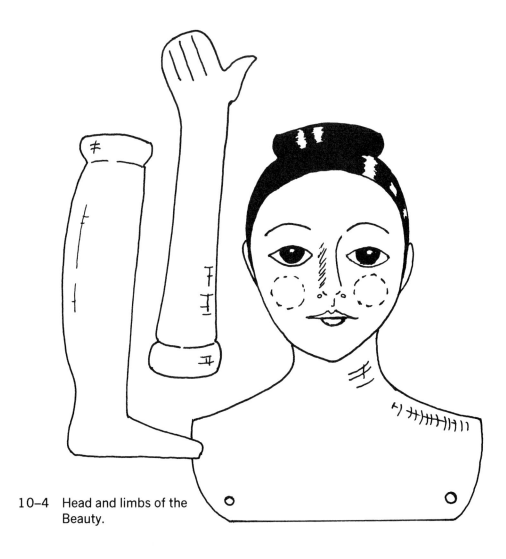

10–4 Head and limbs of the Beauty.

A lump of wedged clay that meets the above
    standards for the shoulder-plate head and lower
    arms of the Beast/Prince
Bisque stains and sealer

Following the procedures outlined in Chapter Nine, model the parts of the dolls. Figure 10-4 illustrates basic structure of the head and limbs of the Beauty. Specific information relating to the shape of the features of the Beast/Prince can be obtained by referring to the drawing of the Beast (fig. 10-5) and the photograph of the Prince (fig. 10-6).

Here are a few additional aids. Build the shoulder plates solidly so they will support the weight of the wet clay heads. Wait to hollow out the shoulder plates until the clay is leather-hard. Beauty's hands can be modeled cupped, but model the hands of the Beast/Prince flat and symmetrical. They should appear identical front or back. Also, because these dolls are original and one of a kind and we do not intend to make molds, the modeling can be ornate. There is no need to worry about undercuts. Projections, grooves, and crevices

10–6   The head of the Prince.

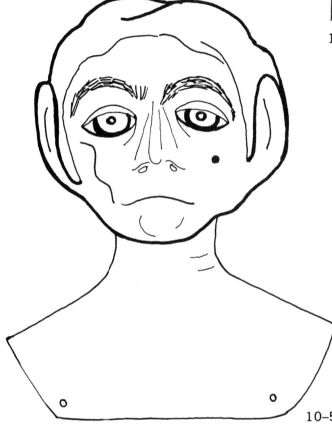

10–5   The Beast's head.

in the surface of the clay can be employed if they enhance the appearance of the work. Last, model both dolls and their limbs simultaneously to maintain proper proportions.

These dolls do not have wigs; their hair is modeled of clay and painted. Beauty's hairstyle is quite simple, an old-fashioned bun encircling the top of her head. The hair of the Beast/Prince serves as a dividing line between the two faces. It is modeled to fan out around the features of each face and conceal one from the other. Refer again to the illustrations and photographs for additional information.

Model a lip and a crevice encircling the base of each bisque limb (fig. 10-4).

When the general structure of the heads, with the hair and the features, is modeled to your satisfaction, smooth the surface of the clay and begin the drying process. Set the pieces on wooden slats and cover their upper surfaces with damp pieces of cotton sheeting (fig. 9-4). Take particular care to keep slender projections from the surface of the clay damp. These areas (fingers, ears, etc.) will dry more quickly than the main body of the clay and may crack.

When the pieces are leather-hard (in a day or two, depending on humidity), they can be hollowed out. Use a modeling tool with a loop end (fig. 9-5) and scoop out the interior of each piece. The walls of these small models should be no thicker than ½ inch. Leather-hard clay pieces can be sliced in half to make hollowing out easier. Make a clean cut, slicing the clay into two equal segments. When you are finished, put the pieces back together following the procedure for mending a broken piece (Chapter Nine). Carefully smooth and seal the seam with a wooden modeling tool. No sign of the joint should be visible.

The leather-hard stage is also the stage at which to punch holes in the shoulder plates for later attachment to the fabric body. Punch one hole in each of the four corners of the plate. If the clay requires any additional carving, do it now. Smooth the surface with a piece of nylon stocking.

Allow the clay doll parts ten days to two weeks to become bone dry.

Bisque-fire the bone-dry pieces to cone 06 (1859° Fahrenheit).

If necessary, polish the fired surface of the clay with extrafine sandpaper or a fine grit scrubber. Wear a protective mask. Clean away any grit or dust that remains on the clay surface.

The doll parts can now be colored with bisque stain. The head and limbs of Beauty, the lower arms and the Prince-half of the multiface head are first coated with a color of bisque stain called "dresden flesh." The paint is scrubbed into the surface of the clay with a bristle brush. One careful application is sufficient. You can mix your own flesh color by combining red and white. Add a dab of yellow or blue to the mixture, depending on the tone of flesh you are seeking. The face of the Beast is stained deep brown. Add a touch of black to bright red for the correct color.

Refer again to the photographs and illustrations of the faces of the three dolls as guides for painting hair and features. Lightly sketch (with a pencil) the hairline and features of each face before proceeding with the brush. Paint the hair of both dolls black. Paint the eyebrows, the outline of the eye, and the iris and slenderly outline the mouth of Beauty with black paint. Obtain a pale rose color of stain by mixing white, bright red, and a drop of blue. Paint the nostrils, lips, and the line inside each ear with this color. Also paint the cheeks, but apply the paint sparingly, and blend it over the surface of the cheek with a soft cotton cloth. Paint the whites of Beauty's eyes and add a dot of white paint to each iris for a highlight. Paint the brows of the Prince and the outline of his eyes and delicately outline his mouth with black. Add a touch of yellow and a little more white to the rose mixture, causing it to become a warm, pale orange. Paint the lips, nostrils, ear line, and a dot at the inner corner of each eye with this color of paint. Paint the cheek patches, blending the color with a cloth. Paint the irises of the Prince's eyes bright blue. Paint the whites and add a highlight to each of his eyes. Paint the Beast's eyebrows, the outline of his eyes, his mole and scar, black. Mix red and yellow and add a touch of black, for a strong shade of orange, and use it to paint the lips, nostrils, and the ear lines of the Beast. Also run a line of this color beside the black line to accent the scar. Paint his eyes bright green (mix yellow and blue). Paint the whites and add a highlight to each eye.

When the stain is dry, coat each doll part with two thin applications of sealer. Allow the first coat to dry before applying the second.

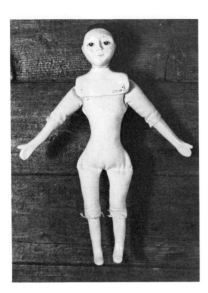

10–7   Beauty's body.

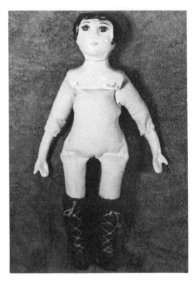

10–8   The body of the Beast/
Prince.

The Fabric Bodies

The fabric bodies of the Beauty and Beast/Prince are constructed of Kettle Cloth. This fabric is a fifty-fifty blend of cotton and polyester. It is sturdy without being heavy, making it an excellent choice of body fabric. The Beast's boots are permanently attached, at the knee, to the cloth body. They were cut from brown fake fur.

Materials

⅓ yard of flesh-colored fabric from which to cut the
    bodies of both dolls
A 12 x 16-inch piece of brown fake fur fabric for
    boots
A skein of bright yellow embroidery thread for boot
    laces and claws
White glue
Embroidery thread or sturdy string for attaching the
    bisque to the fabric
Thread to match the fabric
¼ pound of polyester stuffing

Using the patterns (figs. 10-9, 10-10) as a guide, cut two body pieces for each doll and four boots from the fabrics you have chosen. Transfer all markings to the right side of the fabrics.

Stitch together the Beauty's body first. Begin by stitching the entire shoulder seam from one elbow edge to the opposite edge (fig. 10-11). Turn to the inside ¼ inch of fabric along the base of each arm. Stitch close to the edge of these folded pieces, forming casing for drawstrings (fig. 6-21). Stitch the crotch seam. Press to the inside ¼ inch of fabric along the lower edge of each leg. Stitch close to the edge of these folded pieces, again creating casings for drawstrings. Stitch the side seams, leaving an opening between one set of notches. Do not stitch the ends of the casing closed. Turn the body right side out.

Thread a drawstring through each casing. A 7-inch length of embroidery thread or sturdy string will do for each drawstring. Leave sufficient string dangling from each casing to tie in a sturdy knot.

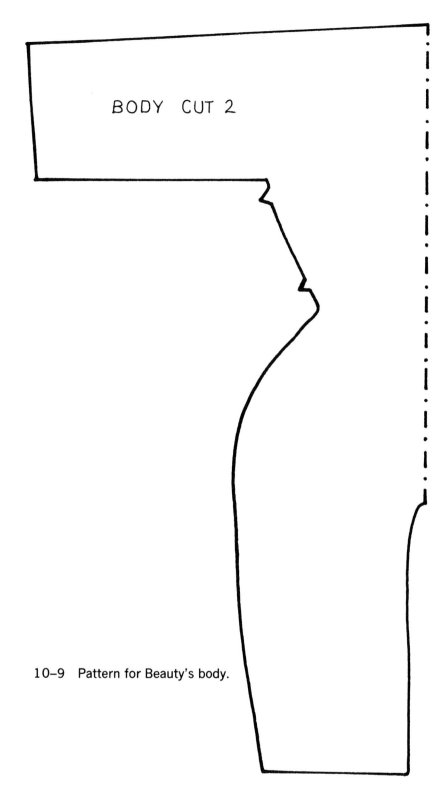

BODY CUT 2

10-9   Pattern for Beauty's body.

The bisque limbs of Beauty can now be attached to the fabric body. To begin, coat the lip above the groove of one arm with white glue. Slip the arm inside the body through the side opening. Try to keep the glue from coming in contact with the fabric. Slip the bisque hand out through the elbow opening of the arm to which you plan to attach the piece. The base of the clay arm is wider than the fabric opening. The fabric should retain the bisque piece, prevent-

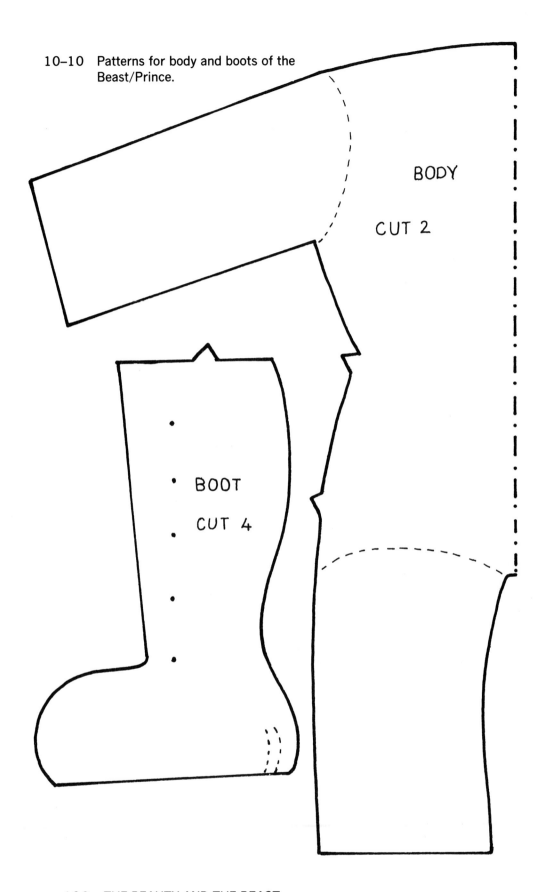

10–10 Patterns for body and boots of the
Beast/Prince.

BODY

CUT 2

BOOT

CUT 4

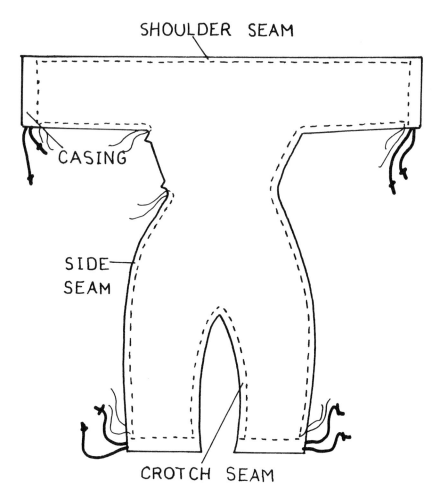

SHOULDER SEAM

CASING

SIDE SEAM

CROTCH SEAM

10–11 Stitching together the body.

ing it from slipping out of the body. Draw up the drawstring (so it nestles in the groove below the lip of the arm) and tie it in a sturdy knot. Add a drop of glue to each knot to prevent its coming untied. Follow this same procedure and attach a bisque arm to the opposite fabric arm and the bisque legs to the fabric legs. Thumbs should point away from the body, and the toes of the feet should face forward.

Now, stuff the upper arms and upper legs above the bisque. Use small bits of stuffing to prevent lumps. The upper limbs should be soft and flexible when stuffed. End stuffing 1 inch below the dotted stitching lines marked at the shoulders and hips of the body. Machine stitch across each of these lines to create joints.

Last, stuff the torso. It should be firm and resilient to support the weight of the head. Turn ¼ inch of fabric along the side opening edges to the inside. By hand, stitch the edges securely closed.

To attach the shoulder plate of the head to the body, loosely stitch an 8-inch length of embroidery thread or sturdy string through the fabric of the body and out each hole in the bisque shoulder (fig. 10-12). Leave the ends of the string dangling. Tip up the head, taking care not to pull the threads out of the holes, and coat the inside of the shoulder plate with white glue. Press the shoulder plate against the body. Draw up the strings and tie each in a sturdy knot. Place a drop of glue on each knot to hold it in place. Stretch a rubber band over the head and between the legs of the doll to hold the head tightly in

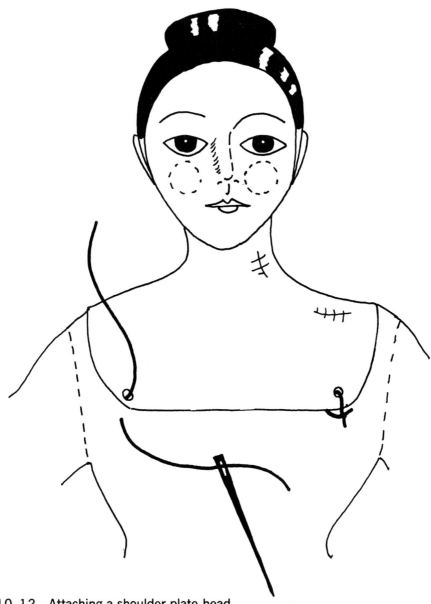

10–12 Attaching a shoulder-plate head.

position until the glue is dry. Beauty's body is assembled.

The Beast's body varies from Beauty's only because he has fabric feet. Stitch his body in exactly the same way as Beauty's, but skip the casings on the base of the legs. Turn the body right side out.

With right sides of the fabric together, stitch the perimeter of each pair of boot pieces together, leaving the notched upper edge unstitched (fig. 10-13A). Turn the boots right side out. Turn ¼ inch of fabric along the upper

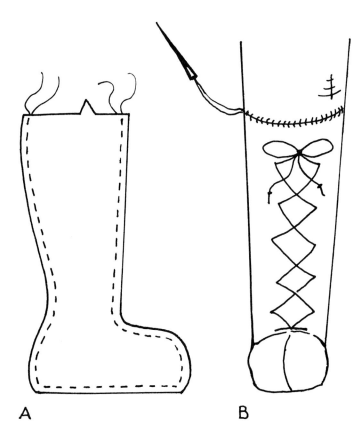

10–13 A. Stitching together a boot.
B. Attaching a boot to the
base of a leg.

edge of one boot and the lower edge of one leg, to the inside. By hand, using small carefully concealed stitches, stitch the upper edge of the boot to the lower edge of the body leg (fig. 10-13B). Repeat and attach the second boot to the remaining leg.

Attach the bisque arms. Stuff the upper arms, boots, and upper legs. Stitch joints and stuff the torso, stitching the side opening closed exactly as you did for Beauty. Attach the shoulder plate, also following the same instructions. Be sure the face of the Prince faces the same direction as the toes of the boots. To finish the body, embroider claws over the dotted lines marked on the heel of the boot. Stitch crisscrossed embroidery-thread laces up the front of each boot, using the dots marked on the fabric as guides. The Beast/Prince is assembled. Both dolls are now ready to dress.

The Clothing

Beauty is dressed to look like a princess. She wears a full-skirted, long-sleeved gown of purple brocade highlighted by metallic gold threads. Lace decorates the neckline and a black velvet sash girdles the waist of the gown. Beauty also wears an off-white satin slip that is stiffened and made full with net fabric. The base of the slip is edged with lace. Her pantalets are white cotton decorated with lace. Beauty's outfit is completed by the addition of a pair of black felt boots and spats.

The Beast/Prince has two sides to his clothing. First of all, he wears a full-length, hooded, fur cloak. Beneath the cloak is a long-sleeved, V-necked shirt, laced at the throat with embroidery thread. The Beast's side of the shirt is cut from somber black and white print cotton. The Prince's side is pale blue satin. The Beast's side of the pantaloons are a coarse cotton weave displaying black, brown, and ocher stripes. The Prince's side of the pantaloons are navy-blue panne velvet. The doll's underpants are white cotton. You can use these fabrics or choose others. A list of materials necessary to make the clothing for both dolls follows.

10–14 Beauty's clothing.

Materials

BEAUTY

¼ yard of fabric for Beauty's gown
A rectangle of fabric 6½ x 17 inches for the slip
A rectangle of net fabric 12 x 16 inches to stiffen
    the slip
A scrap of cotton fabric measuring 6 x 10 inches
    for the pantalets
One yard of ½-inch-wide gathered lace edging
Two 5-inch lengths of ¼-inch-wide elastic
An 8 x 8-inch scrap of felt for the boots and spats
4 white sequins
6 tiny snap closures

BEAST/PRINCE

A 14 x 16-inch piece of imitation fur fabric for the
   cloak and hood
An 11 x 14-inch rectangle of black satin lining fabric
   for the interior of the cloak
Two 7 x 12-inch pieces of fabric, one for each side
   of the shirt
Two 7 x 9-inch pieces of fabric, one for each side of
   the pantaloons
A 5 x 10-inch piece of fabric for the underpants
Black embroidery thread for the shirt laces
A 26-inch length of ¼-inch-wide elastic
A 22-inch length of ⅛-inch gold braid for a cloak tie

Thread to match all the fabrics

Use the patterns (figs. 10-15, 10-16, 10-17, 10-18) as guides and cut the
necessary pieces from the fabrics you have chosen. Cut a rectangle of fabric
measuring 8 x 18 inches for the skirt of the dress. Cut a rectangle of fabric
measuring 6½ x 17 inches for the slip and four 4 x 10½-inch rectangles of
net fabric. Stitch the narrow ends of the net together forming one 40-inch
length. Cut a rectangle of imitation fur fabric measuring 11 x 14 inches for
the cloak. Cut another rectangle 11 x 14 inches to line the cloak. Transfer all
markings to the wrong side of the fabric.
   THE PANTALETS. Align the two pantalet pieces. Stitch together one side
from the waist edge to the base of the leg. Open out the piece. Turn ½ inch of
fabric along the waist edge to the inside. Press. Stitch close to the raw edge of
this folded piece, forming a casing for elastic (fig. 6-21). Thread a 4½-inch
length of ¼-inch elastic through the casing. Stitch the elastic securely to both
ends of the casing. Stitch the second side seam of the pantalets from the base
of the leg to the waist edge, stitching the ends of the casing securely together
(fig. 7-13). Turn and press to the inside ¼ inch of fabric along the base of
each leg. Stitch these folded edges in place. Cut two 3½-inch lengths of gathered lace edging. Stitch a piece of lace to the base of each leg. Stitch the
crotch seam, stitching together the ends of the lace as you do so. Turn the
pantalets right side out and press.
   THE SLIP. To begin, turn ¼ inch of fabric along one long edge of the rectangle of fabric to the inside. Press and stitch this edge in place. Stitch a 17-inch
piece of gathered lace edging over this hem. Next, make a casing for the elastic by turning ½ inch of fabric along the opposite long edge to the inside. Press
and stitch close to the raw edge (fig. 6-21). Now, baste ⅛ inch within the long
edge of the entire length of the rectangle of net fabric. Draw up the basting
stitches, tightly gathering the net, so the edge measures 17 inches. Pin the
gathered edge of the net to the wrong side of the slip, 2 inches below waist
edge. Adjust the gathers so the net extends the width of the slip. Stitch the
gathered edge of the net to the slip, placing the line of stitching ¼ inch within
the edge of the net. Thread a 5-inch length of elastic through the casing. Stitch
both ends to the casing. To finish, stitch the two short ends of the slip together
from the waist edge to the base of the lace, catching in the net. Turn the slip
right side out and press it carefully so as not to scorch the net.
   THE GOWN. Stitch the bodice front to the two bodice back pieces along the
shoulder seams (fig. 7-14). Turn and press ½ inch of fabric along the back
opening edges to the inside. Stitch these edges in place. Hem the edge of the
neck. Stitch an 8-inch length of ½-inch-wide gathered lace edging to the inside
of the neck edge. Hem the raw ends of the lace.

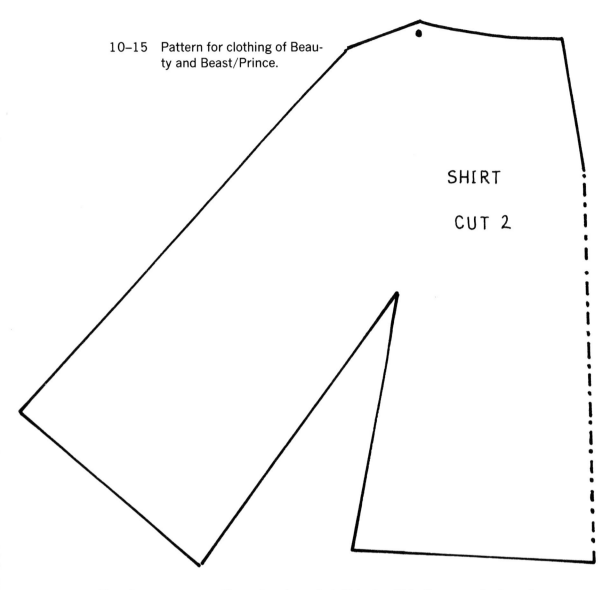

10–15 Pattern for clothing of Beauty and Beast/Prince.

SHIRT

CUT 2

The sleeves are next. Run a basting stitch ⅛ inch within the curved edge of each sleeve. Draw up the stitching so the sleeve is slightly gathered. Pin and then baste a sleeve to each armhole opening. Adjust the gathers to fit the armhole. Stitch the sleeves to the bodice.

Stitch the underarm seams of the bodice from the base to the wrist ends of the sleeves. Hem the ends of the sleeves.

To attach the skirt to the bodice, begin by stitching a line of basting ⅛ inch within one long edge of the rectangle of skirt fabric (fig. 8-15). Now, draw up the basting thread so the skirt is gathered. With right sides together, pin the gathered edge of the skirt to the lower edge of the bodice, with the back edges of the skirt overlapping the bodice by ½ inch. Adjust the gathers so they are uniform. Baste and then stitch the skirt to the bodice. Stitch the back of the skirt together from the lower edge to within 1 inch of the waist of the bodice (fig. 10-19). Hem the back opening edges of the skirt below the waist. Hem the base of the skirt. Stitch two small snap closures to the neck and waist of the back opening edges of the gown. Press the completed gown.

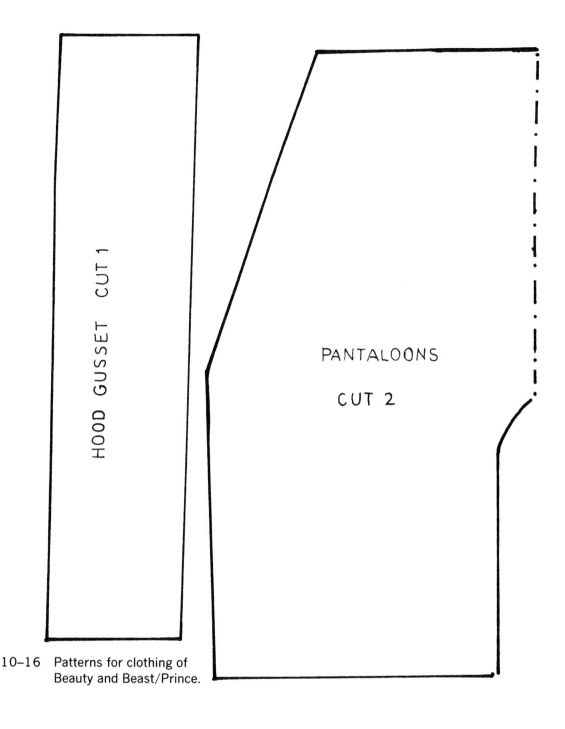

HOOD GUSSET CUT 1

PANTALOONS

CUT 2

10–16 Patterns for clothing of
Beauty and Beast/Prince.

THE BOOTS AND SPATS. To begin, use the sole pattern as a guide and cut
two soles from lightweight cardboard. Trim ¼ inch from the perimeter of each.
Cut two cardboard heels and trim ⅛ inch from the perimeter of each. Glue
(white glue or liquid latex) a cardboard insert to each felt sole and heel. Glue
the cardboard side of one heel to the felt side of each sole. Stitch together the
toe seam between the dots marked on the fabric of each felt upper. Stitch together the heel seams along the notched edge. Turn the uppers right side out.
Overcast-stitch the base of a felt upper to the sole of each shoe (fig. 8-13).
The cardboard insert should be on the inside.

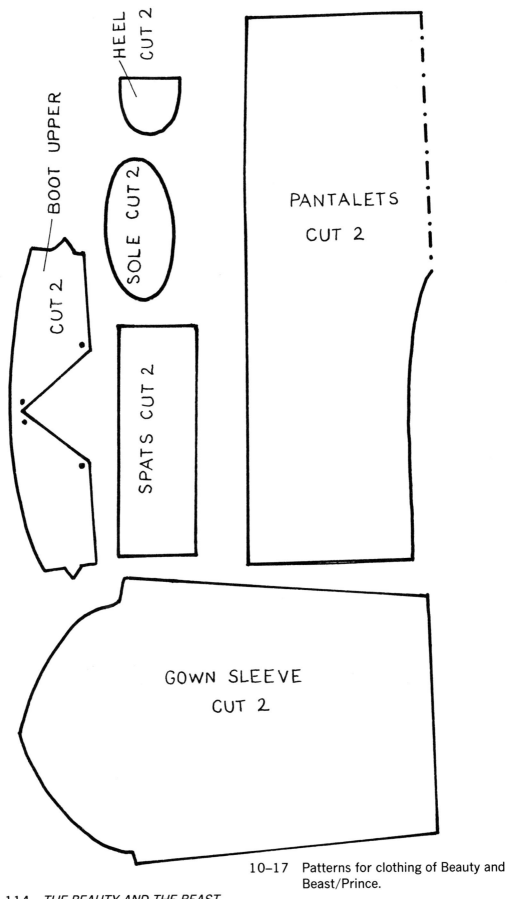

HEEL
CUT 2

BOOT UPPER

CUT 2

SOLE CUT 2

PANTALETS

CUT 2

SPATS CUT 2

GOWN SLEEVE

CUT 2

10–17 Patterns for clothing of Beauty and Beast/Prince.

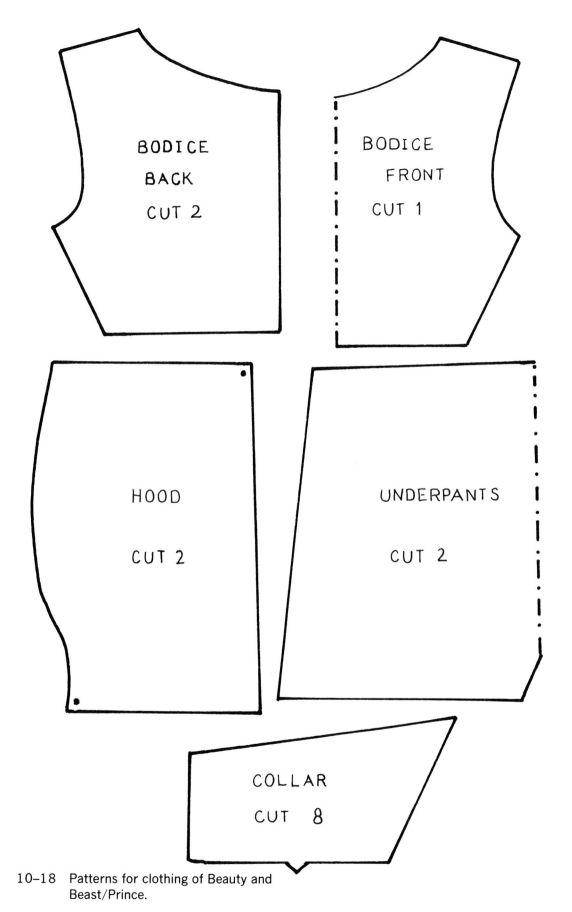

10-18 Patterns for clothing of Beauty and Beast/Prince.

The spats are simply rectangles of felt that snap around the doll's ankles and slide over the upper edge of her boots. They could also be cut from white felt if you wish a contrast. Stitch two snap closures ⅛ inch within the narrow end of the felt piece, placing one in each corner. As a decoration, glue a white sequin on the right side of the fabric, over each snap. Place the boots on the doll, and snap the spats around her ankles.

The Beauty's clothes are complete. We will go on to those of the Beast/Prince.

THE UNDERPANTS. Stitch together one side seam of the pair of underpant pieces, from the base of one leg to the waist edge. Open out the piece. Turn ½ inch of fabric along the waist edge to the inside. Fold and press the edge in place. Stitch close to the raw edge of the folded piece, forming a casing for elastic (fig. 6-21). Thread a 7-inch length of ¼-inch-wide elastic through the casing. Stitch it securely to both ends of the casing. Stitch the second side seam. Stitch the crotch seam. Hem the base of the legs. Turn the piece right side out and press.

THE SHIRT. Stitch together the shoulder edge of the two shirt pieces from the waist ends of the sleeves to the dots marked on the neck edge. Hem the front edges of the V on both sides of the shirt. Now, attach the collar. First, stitch together the eight collar pieces so you have four pieces, half of them one kind of fabric and half another kind of fabric (fig. 10-20). Next, align two half-and-half pieces and press ¼ inch of fabric along one notched edge to the wrong side. Match fabrics on each end. Stitch the perimeter of the pieces together, but not the notched edge (fig. 8-14). Turn the collar right side out and press. With right sides together, matching collar and shirt fabrics, baste and then stitch the unfolded edge of the collar fabric to one side of the shirt. Press the seam toward the collar. Stitch the pressed edge of the collar over the seam. Repeat, assembling and attaching the second collar piece to the opposite side of the shirt.

Stitch the underarm seams of the shirt. Hem the ends of the sleeves and the base of the shirt. Press. Put the shirt on the doll. Stitch crisscrossed embroidery-thread laces up the front of the V opening on each side of the shirt. Tie the laces in a bow.

THE PANTALOONS. Align and stitch together one side seam of the pantaloon pieces, from the base of the leg to the waist edge. Open out the piece. Turn and press ½ inch of fabric along the waist edge to the inside. Stitch close to the edge of this folded piece, forming a casing for elastic (fig. 6-21). Thread an 8-inch length of ¼-inch elastic through this casing. Stitch the elastic securely to both ends of the casing. Stitch the second side seam. Open out each leg. Turn and press ½-inch of fabric to the inside along the base of each leg. Stitch, forming a casing for elastic. Thread a 5-inch length of ¼-inch-wide elastic through each casing, stitching the ends securely to the casing. Stitch the crotch seam. Turn the pantaloons right side out and press.

THE CLOAK. With right sides together, stitch the cloak lining to the cloak fabric, placing the line of stitching ¼ inch within the outer edge of the fabric. Leave a 2-inch opening. Turn the cloak right side out through the opening. Press, pressing ¼ inch of fabric along the opening edges to the inside. Top-stitch ⅛ inch within the perimeter of the cloak, top-stitching the opening edges together as you do so.

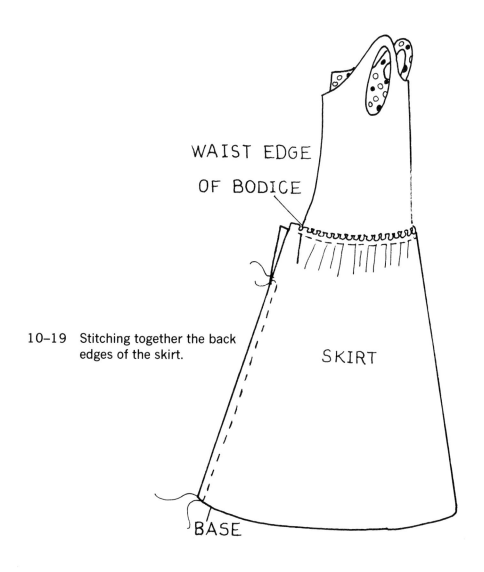

WAIST EDGE
OF BODICE

SKIRT

BASE

10–19 Stitching together the back
edges of the skirt.

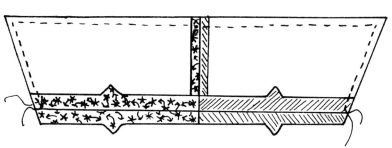

10–20   Assembling the collar.

Run a line of basting stitches ¼ inch within and the length of one short end of the cloak. Draw up the stitches gathering the edge of the cloak to 4 inches. Stitch over the gathers, holding them permanently in place.

With right sides together, stitch one side of the gusset to one hood piece, between the dots. Stitch the second hood piece to the opposite side of the gusset. Hem the edges of the hood that are not notched. With furry sides together, pin, baste, and then stitch the notched edge of the hood to the gathered edge of the cloak. Press the seam toward the hood. Stitch the gold braid over the seam with an equal portion extending from each side of the cloak for ties. Press the cloak and the Beast/Prince's clothing is completed.

CHAPTER 11
Project Five-Thumbelina

11-2 Thumbelina.

11-1 Thumbelina in the flower.

She kissed the petals and the flower burst open. In the middle of the blossom, on the soft velvety petals, sat a tiny girl, delicate and pretty. She was scarcely as big as a thumb, so they called her Thumbelina.

Hans Christian Andersen

Thumbelina is a tiny, all-bisque baby doll. She has set-in blown-glass eyes and a curly mohair wig. The little doll is nestled in a felt flower, covered with a green felt leaf. She wears white cotton diapers, plush booties, a satin slip, a pink dotted-swiss dress, a pale blue plush cape and a matching bonnet with a lace brim. The doll is 6 inches tall. Her head has a circumference of 4½ inches.

Modeling

If you have not already done so, read Chapter Nine, which contains basic information concerning modeling, drying, firing, and staining bisque. Remember, clay shrinks as much as 20 percent during drying and firing, so plan your

119

model accordingly. A list of materials necessary to make one 6-inch all-bisque doll follows.

Materials

Approximately two pounds of wedged modeling clay,
  which matures white or near-white at cone 06,
  to model the head, torso, arms, and legs of
  Thumbelina
Bisque stains and sealer

Figure 11-4 is a photograph of Thumbelina's body. Use it as a guide when shaping the parts of the doll body.

Work on all parts of the doll simultaneously to keep the pieces in proportion to one another. Model round protrusions on the ends of limbs (fig. 5-9). These joints will fit inside the torso. Be sure to model a torso with ample breadth to hold the base of the limbs. Last of all, because the doll has set-in eyes, slice off the top of her head (fig. 9-3). A handy tool for this job is a fettling knife (fig. 11-3B).

When you are satisfied with construction and modeling, smooth the clay surface.

Begin the drying process by placing the parts of the doll on wooden slats, raised above the work surface (fig. 9-4). Cover the upper surface of each piece with a damp cloth. Pay particular attention to the rate at which tiny projections, such as ears and fingers, dry. Keep them misted with a fine spray of water until the larger pieces are almost dry.

When the head and torso are leather-hard, scoop the clay out of their interiors with a loop-ended modeling tool (fig. 9-5). Continue until the pieces are hollow and the walls are a uniform ½ inch in thickness. Use calipers, dividers, a compass, or a template of small circles to gauge the diameter of the base of the neck and limbs. Add ⅛ inch to each limb measurement. The neck should fit almost exactly into the socket. Draw circles, using these measurements, on the torso where the sockets will be. Cut out the sockets with a sharp feather knife. (fig. 11-3A).

It is not necessary to hollow the arms and legs. They are small enough to be fired solid. Do, however, make a hole through the center of each rounded projection at the base of the limbs. The holes must be clear and large enough (remember shrinkage) to thread elastic cord in one side and out the other. A lace tool (fig. 11-3C) can be used for this job.

Now, cut a hole slightly larger than a penny in the top of the doll's head (fig. 7-5). This hole will be necessary when it comes time to set the eyes. Next, cut two identical almond-shaped eye sockets which are slightly larger (again taking shrinkage into consideration) than the projected eye sockets. This procedure is explained in detail in Chapter Seven. Cut out the eye sockets with a sharp feather knife. Gently smooth the inside edges of the cuts.

Do any additional trimming and/or carving that you feel is necessary. Smooth the clay surfaces with a piece of nylon stocking.

Allow the pieces to become bone dry. Control the process. It will take a week to ten days.

Fire the bone-dry clay to cone 06 (1859° Fahrenheit).

Polish the cooled, fired surface of the head, torso, and limbs with extrafine sandpaper or a fine grit scrubber. Wear a protective face mask to prevent inhalation of the dust. Clean the surfaces of the pieces.

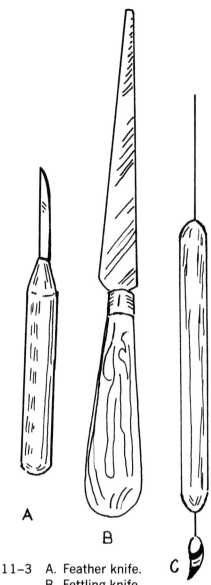

11-4   The body of
Thumbelina.

A

B

C

11-3   A. Feather knife.
       B. Fettling knife.
       C. Lace tool.

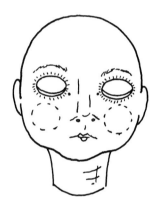

11-5   Thumbelina's face.

Paint the head, limbs, and torso of the doll with a flesh color of bisque stain. You can use premixed flesh color or mix your own. Scrub this first coat of stain well into the surface of the bisque, using a bristle brush. Refer to figure 11-5, a sketch of Thumbelina's face. Use it as a guide and lightly sketch the features on the head. Use a tiny brush (000) and paint reddish-brown eyebrows. Paint tiny lashes surrounding the eye sockets. Paint the inside edges of the eye sockets. Also, delicately outline the mouth and nostrils with this color. Mix a warm rose (white, red, and a hint of blue) color of stain. Paint the inside of the lips, nostrils, and ear line with this mixture. Then apply a hint of rose to the cheeks, gently blending it over the surface.

When the stain is dry, coat the doll parts with two layers of sealer. Allow one coat to dry before applying the second coat.

Setting the Eyes

Thumbelina's eyes are tiny, round, blue-gray blown-glass eyes with an outside diameter of ¼ inch. It is always a good idea to have pairs of eyes, one size larger and one size smaller, on hand in case the eye sockets shrink or change shape during drying and firing.

The eyes are set in a bisque doll head following the same procedure for setting eyes in a composition head. Refer to Project Two, The Snow Queen, for a detailed description of the process.

You will need the following materials.

Materials

One pair of blown-glass eyes (approximate outside
    diameter ¼ inch)
Rubber cement
Sculpta Mold ©
A cork with a ¾-inch diameter
White glue

Coat the inside of each eye socket with rubber cement. Place the glass eyes in the sockets, positioning them carefully. Mix 1 tablespoon of Sculpta Mold with ½ tablespoon of water. Pack this material around the portions of the glass eyes that are inside the head. Press the eyes tightly into the sockets. Allow the compound several minutes to dry. Clean rubber cement off the surface of the eyes with a toothpick or similar tool.

The cork is used to plug the hole in the top of the doll's head. Check to see if it fits tightly into the opening. When it is in place, its exposed end will be level with the clay surface of the head. The majority of the cork will be inside the head. Trim the cork for a correct fit. Coat it with white glue. Push the cork into position in the head. Allow the glue to dry. Buckram circles can be purchased from doll-parts suppliers. These can be glued over the hole and substituted for the cork.

Assembling the Doll

Thumbelina's system of jointing and assemblage is similar to that used for Hansel and Gretel (Chapter Eight). Read the portion of that chapter describing this procedure. Also, refer to figure 8-7.

Materials

A 10-inch length of round elastic cord
One popsicle stick or pencil
Clear nail polish
White glue

Bisque limbs, when moved, have a tendency to scrape and grate against their sockets. To prevent this, coat the base of each limb, where it comes in contact with the torso socket, with clear nail polish. Allow this application to become hard and dry before proceeding.

Begin stringing the doll by threading elastic through the hole in the top side of one arm and drawing it out the bottom side. Leave 2 inches of the end of the strand projecting from the top side. Push the elastic that extends from the underside of the arm through the socket into the interior of the body. Then, place the base of the arm (including the 2-inch strand) into the socket. Draw the long piece of elastic through the torso and out the leg socket directly below the arm. Thread the elastic through the top side of the leg that fits in this socket and out the bottom side. Place the elastic and the base of the leg in the torso socket. Draw the elastic across the base of the body and out the opposite leg socket. Thread the elastic through the hole in the underside of this leg and out the top side. Insert the elastic and the leg into the socket. Draw the elastic up through the body and out the remaining arm socket. Thread the elastic through the hole in the bottom side of this arm and out the top side. Place the elastic and the arm in the socket.

Lay a popsicle stick or pencil across the neck opening (fig. 8-7). Draw the ends of the elastic up, out of the torso, on either side of the stick. Pull up the cord, tightly settling each limb in its socket. Knot the cord firmly over the stick. Remove the stick and let the knot drop back into the torso.

Last, coat the neck of the head with white glue. Place it in its socket. Position the head before the glue dries. When the glue is dry, assembly is complete.

The Wig

Thumbelina's wig is made of reddish-brown mohair yarn. The yarn is twisted around wooden dowel sticks, soaked with water, and allowed to dry. This process curls the yarn. The curls are stitched to a small fabric circle which is then glued to the doll's head. There is more information about mohair in Chapter Six (subsection: "The Wig"). To make Thumbelina's wig, you need the following materials.

Materials

Approximately 3 yards of mohair yarn
A wooden dowel stick with a ⅛-inch diameter
One fabric circle with a diameter of 2¼ inches, which
    is as close to the color of the yarn as possible
White glue
Thread to match the fabric

To begin, curl the yarn. Tie one end of the 3-foot strand of mohair to the wooden dowel stick (fig. 11-6). Wrap the yarn tightly around the stick, proceeding along the length of the dowel. If you have more yarn than stick, wrap a second layer over the first. Tie the end of the yarn tightly around the dowel. Leave the end dangling so you will know where to begin unwrapping. Soak the yarn-covered stick with water. Lay it in an inch of water in the bathtub or soak it under the faucet. Be sure the water penetrates and the yarn is thoroughly wetted. Then, allow the yarn to dry.

When the yarn is dry, make the wig. Begin by running a line of basting stitches ⅛ inch within and around the perimeter of the fabric circle. Leave the ends of the thread dangling. Unwrap the yarn from the dowel stick and cut curls, as

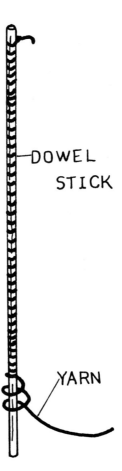

11–6　Curling mohair yarn.

DOWEL STICK

YARN

you need them, 3 to 5 inches in length. Stitch a row of curls around the perimeter of the fabric circle. Stitch the center of each curled strand securely to the fabric with carefully concealed hand stitches. Stitch short curls to the front of the wig. They should be just long enough to touch the doll's forehead. Stitch a second row of curls inside the first. Continue this process, stitching a row inside the last row until you have covered the fabric with an overlapping layer of curls. Next, draw up the basting stitches, slightly cupping the fabric of the wig. Coat the crown of the doll's head with glue, covering the general area indicated in figure 6-4. Press the fabric over the glue. Hold the wig tightly to the doll's head with rubber bands until the glue dries.

When the glue is dry, trim the curls if necessary. For a finishing touch, tie a strand of ⅛-inch gold braid around Thumbelina's head for a headband.

The Clothing

Thumbelina wears traditional baby-doll clothing. This includes a cotton diaper, booties, and a bonnet. Her dress is pink dotted-swiss and has long sleeves and a long skirt. It is tied at the waist with a sash of gold braid. If you prefer, make the dress of white lace and it will look like a christening gown. She also wears a full satin slip. Her cape is cut from blue, short-napped plush fabric as are her bonnet and booties. The cape is lined with blue satin. You can, of course, substitute other fabrics.

11–7   Thumbelina's clothing.

Materials

A 12 x 12-inch square of fabric for the cape,
     booties, and bonnet
A 4½ x 8½-inch rectangle of fabric to line the cape
An 8 x 11-inch rectangle of fabric for the slip
A 12 x 12-inch rectangle of fabric for the dress
A 3½ x 4½-inch rectangle of white cotton fabric for
     the diaper
Pink embroidery thread for bootie and bonnet ties
A 4½-inch strand of ½-inch-wide gathered lace
     edging for the bonnet brim
A 15-inch length of ⅛-inch-wide satin ribbon for
     cape ties
4 tiny snap closures
Thread to match the fabrics

Using the patterns (fig. 11-8) as guides, cut the number of pieces indicated
from the fabrics you have chosen. You will also need to cut a rectangle of fabric measuring 5½ x 11½ inches for the skirt of the dress; also, one measuring
5 x 11 inches must be cut for the skirt of the slip. Cut a rectangle measuring
4½ x 8½ inches for the cape and one of this same measurement for the cape
lining. Also, cut a rectangle of white cotton measuring 3½ x 4½ inches for the
diaper. Transfer all markings to the wrong sides of the fabrics.

THE DIAPER. Using ¼ inch of fabric, narrowly hem the four edges of the
rectangular piece of diaper fabric. Put the diaper on the doll (hems on the inside) and stitch the upper sides of the piece together with two or three hand
stitches, or pin them in place with tiny safety pins.

THE SLIP. Stitch the front of the bodice to the back, along the shoulder
seams (fig. 7-14). Stitch the underarm seams. Hem the neck edge, the back
opening edges, and the armhole openings.

Run a line of basting stitches ⅛ inch within the edge of one long side of the
rectangular piece of fabric that is the skirt of the slip (fig. 8-15). Draw up this
stitching, gathering the edge. With right sides together, pin the gathered edge
to the waist edge of the bodice, adjusting the gathers to fit. The skirt should
overlap the back edges of the bodice by ½ inch. Stitch the skirt to the bodice.
Stitch (fig. 10-19) the back of the skirt together, from the base to within 1

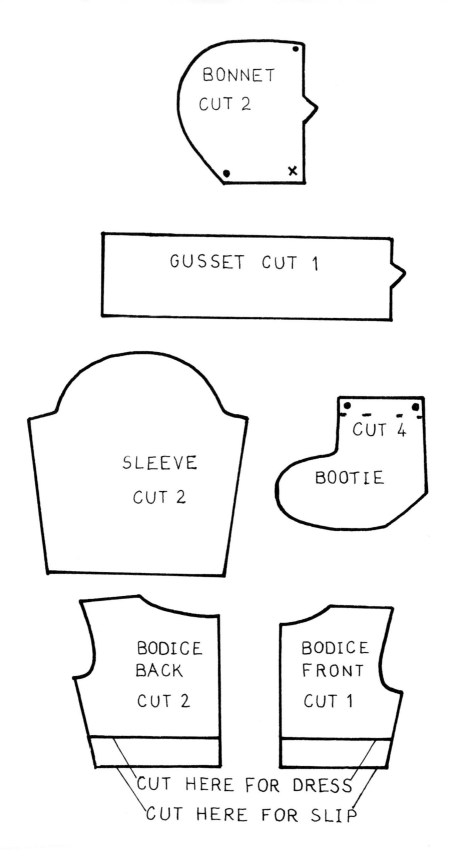

11–8 Patterns for Thumbelina's clothing.

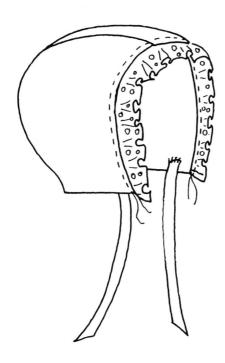

11-9 Stitching lace brim and ribbon ties to the bonnet.

inch of the waist of the bodice. Hem the raw edges below the bodice. Hem the base of the skirt. Stitch a snap closure to the neck and waist of the back opening edges of the bodice. Press the slip.

THE DRESS. Stitch the front of the bodice to the back along the shoulder seams. Hem the neck edge and the back opening edges. Then, insert the sleeves. Run a line of basting ⅛ inch within the curved edge of each sleeve. Draw up the stitching just enough to slightly gather the sleeves. With right sides together, adjusting the gathers, pin and then baste a sleeve to each armhole opening. Stitch the sleeves to the bodice. Stitch the underarm seams from the wrists of the sleeves to the waist edge of the bodice.

Follow the same instructions for attaching the skirt of the dress as for attaching the skirt of the slip. Hem the back opening edges and the base of the dress. Stitch two tiny snap closures to the back opening edges and then press the finished dress. Tie a sash of ⅛-inch gold braid around the waist of the dress.

THE CAPE. To begin, stitch the lining to the cape. With right sides together, align the two pieces and place a line of stitching ¼ inch within the outer edge and around the perimeter. Leave a 2-inch opening. Turn the cape right side out through this opening. Press the piece, pressing ¼ inch of fabric along the opening edges to the inside. Top-stitch ⅛ inch within the edge and around the perimeter of the cape, stitching the open edges closed as you do so.

Place a line of basting stitches ⅛ inch within and the length of one long end of the cape. Draw up these stitches, gathering the edge to a length of 6 inches. Machine stitch over the gathers to make them permanent. Place the piece of satin ribbon over the stitching. An equal length of ribbon should extend from either side of the cape. Stitch the ribbon to the cape. Press the finished cape.

THE BONNET. Align the bonnet gusset with one bonnet piece, matching the dots marked on the fabric. Stitch the gusset to the bonnet (fig. 7-16). Align the opposite side of the bonnet with the unstitched edge of the gusset. Stitch this pair of pieces together, between the dots. Hem the unnotched lower edge of the bonnet. Hem the notched edge. Stitch a piece of gathered lace edging over the notched edge for a bonnet brim (fig. 11-9). Hem the ends of the lace. Stitch embroidery thread ties to the bonnet, through the points marked X on the fabric.

THE BOOTIES. Stitch one pair of bootie pieces together, between the dots (fig. 11-10). Hem the upper edge. Stitch and hem the second bootie. Begin above the toe and stitch a 6-inch strand of embroidery thread in and out of the dashes marked on the fabric near the top of the bootie, ending above the toe. When the bootie is on the doll, draw up the embroidery thread, gathering the bootie around her ankle. Tie the thread in a bow.

With Thumbelina's clothing complete, proceed to her flower bed.

The Flower

Thumbelina rests in a felt flower. She is covered with a green felt leaf. The petals are white felt. The center of the flower is bright orange felt. Pipe cleaners are glued and stitched between the pieces of the petals and leaf. They bend and hold positions. Lines of decorative stitching in contrasting colors give the illusions of veins. Make the flower any color of felt you desire, but be sure to use felt. The edges of the pieces are not hemmed. Felt is a pressed fabric and will not unravel. A list of necessary materials follows.

Materials

⅓ yard of felt for the petals
A piece of felt measuring 5 x 5 inches for the center
    of the flower
A piece of felt measuring 6 x 8 inches for the leaf
20 pipe cleaners
A handful of polyester stuffing
Thread
Liquid latex or fabric glue

Using the patterns for a guide (figs. 11-12, 11-13), cut twelve petals and two leaves from felt. Transfer marking to the right side of the fabrics.

We will begin by assembling the petals. Lay one petal on a flat surface. Arrange three pipe cleaners on the fabric (fig. 11-14A). One by one, lift and coat each pipe cleaner with cloth glue or liquid latex and press it back against the fabric. Align and place a second petal piece over the first. Use a decorative stitch (such as a closely spaced zigzag) and stitch the perimeters of the petal pieces together (fig. 11-14). Then stitch three lines of varying lengths of decorative stitching from the base up toward the tip of the petal. Stitch over the pipe cleaners if they are in your path. Assemble the remaining five petals. Assemble the leaf, following this same procedure. Use a decorative stitch and stitch the veins of the leaf (fig. 11-11).

Lay one center piece on a flat surface. Arrange the six petal pieces around the circumference of the piece (fig. 11-14B). The base of each petal should overlap the center by ½ inch. The sides of the petals may overlap one another. Baste the petals to the circle. Place the second circle over the first with the base of the petals between. Using a closely spaced zigzag stitch, stitch the edges of the circle together, catching the petals between. Stop stitching when a 2-inch opening remains. Fill the center of the flower with polyester stuffing. Stitch the 2-inch opening closed using the same decorative stitch.

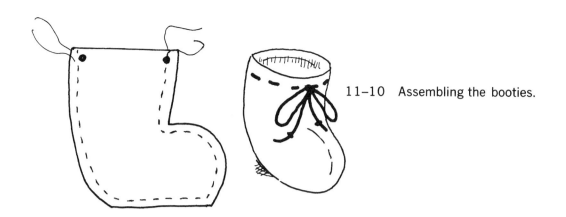

11–10   Assembling the booties.

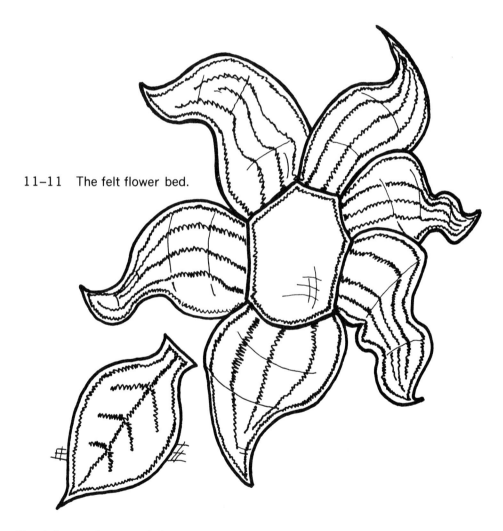

11–11   The felt flower bed.

Bend the petals upward, forming a cup. Stitch the sides of the petals securely to one another, 2 inches above the center of the flower. Bend the tips of the petals into curving, flowerlike positions. Nestle Thumbelina in her flower, covered with the leaf, and Project Five is complete.

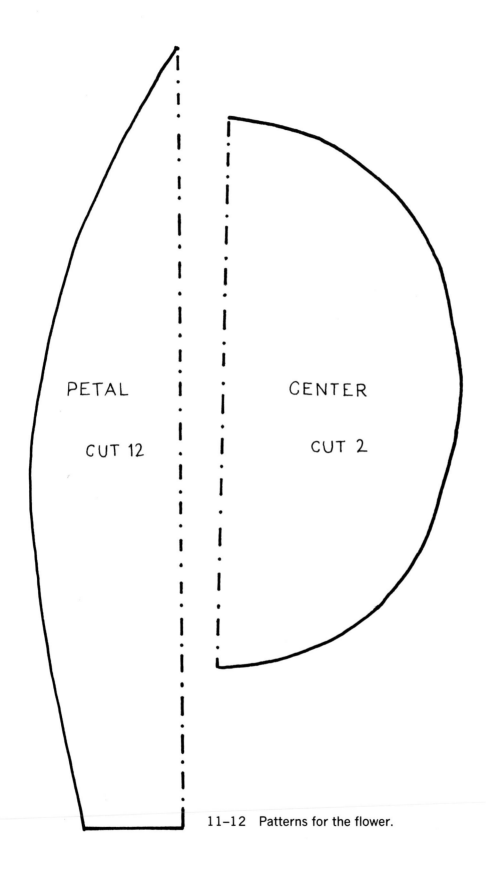

PETAL

CUT 12

CENTER

CUT 2

11-12   Patterns for the flower.

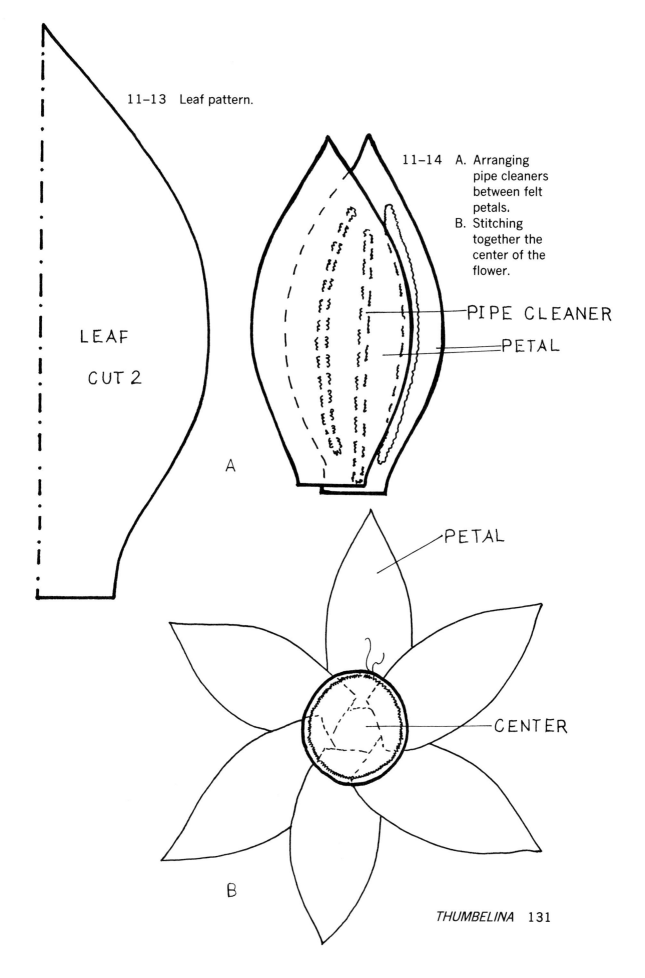

11-13 Leaf pattern.

LEAF

CUT 2

11-14 A. Arranging pipe cleaners between felt petals.
B. Stitching together the center of the flower.

PIPE CLEANER

PETAL

A

PETAL

CENTER

B

THUMBELINA 131

CHAPTER 12
Project Six-The Goose Girl

12-1 The Goose Girl.

Here I am forsaken by all the world, and yet I am a princess. A false waiting-woman brought me to such a pass. She took my royal robes and she took my place with my bridegroom, while I have to do mean service as a goose girl. If my mother knew, it would break her heart in two.

The Brothers Grimm

The Goose Girl has an original, hand-modeled, bisque swivel head. The head is attached to a German ball-jointed, Milvex composition body. The body was purchased from Seeley's Ceramic Service of Oneonta, New York (see Sources of Supply). It is one of several types of composition bodies available to doll artists who wish to put their time and energy into producing just the doll head. The bodies come in sizes from 6 to 19 inches. You can buy bodies designed to look like baby, toddler, child, or adult women. The system of jointing varies from style to style. Most of the bodies are replicas of antique dolls. They were

132

originally developed for craftsmen restoring antique dolls or making reproductions, but are now proving their usefulness to doll artists. The bodies are
flesh-colored and sanded. They can be purchased strung or unstrung. Instructions for stringing are included at a later point in this chapter.

The Goose Girl has brown blown-glass eyes and a brown mohair wig. She is
8½ inches tall. The circumference of her head is 6 inches. She wears a long-
sleeved, ruffle-trimmed, long-skirted dress that combines two colors of delicately printed calico. Her undergarments include a half-slip and cotton panties. She wears white ankle socks and white felt shoes.

Modeling

Before beginning modeling the head of the Goose Girl, read Chapter Nine,
where general information concerning modeling, drying, firing, and staining is
presented. Specific information relating to modeling one swivel head follows.
To begin, you will need these listed materials.

Materials

A ball of wedged modeling clay with a 10-inch
    diameter (The clay should mature white or near-
    white at cone 06.)
Bisque stains and sealer

12–2   The Goose Girl's head.

Refer to figure 12-2, which is a photograph of the Goose Girl's head. Note
the structural aspects of the head that make it unique, and try to reproduce
them when modeling your head. For instance, her eyes are unusually large, her
face is more round than oval, and the forms making up the face (like the nose)
are simplified. Cut off or flatten the top of the head (fig. 9-3).

When modeling the head, take into account the 20-percent shrinkage of clay
during drying and firing. The head is to be attached to a 6-inch body. The circumference of the head after firing is 6 inches. Your wet model should measure approximately 7½ inches. The base of the neck should have a diameter of
approximately 1 inch before firing and just over ¾ inch after firing, to fit into
the socket in the body. The neck socket of the composition body can be
trimmed and enlarged somewhat if necessary.

When you are satisfied with the head, smooth the clay and then begin the drying process. Place the head, raised above the work surface, on wooden slats. Drape a damp piece of cotton sheeting over the model to control drying.

Hollow out the head as soon as it is leather-hard. Use a loop-ended modeling tool (fig. 9-5). The walls of the head should be no more than ½ inch thick, and uniform. Cut a hole 1 inch in diameter in the top of the head (fig. 7-5).

Cut two eye sockets slightly larger than the projected sockets (taking shrinkage into account). Use a sharp feather knife. Refer to Chapter Seven for a more detailed description of this procedure. Smooth the inside edges of the eye sockets.

Smooth the surface of the model with a piece of nylon stocking.

Continue drying the head until it is bone dry. Control the process. It should take a week to ten days.

Bisque-fire the head to cone 06 (1859° Fahrenheit).

Polish the cool head with extrafine sandpaper or a fine grit scrubber. Wear a protective face mask to prevent inhalation of the dust. Clean the surface of the head, removing dust or grit, before proceeding to bisque-staining.

Paint the clay with one thorough coat of flesh-colored bisque stain, scrubbing it into the surface with a bristle brush. There are several premixed flesh colors to choose from, or mix your own.

Next, refer again to the photograph (fig. 12-2). Use it as a guide and lightly sketch the brows, mouth, and lashes on the face. A template featuring small ellipses is useful as a guide to drawing accurate, matching curves, such as eyebrows. Mix bright red bisque stain with a touch of black, achieving a rich, dark brown. Paint slender arching eyebrows. Paint tiny lashes, extending from and rimming the top side of the eye sockets. Paint the inside edges of the eye socket with this color. Use a very delicate line and outline the mouth. Next, mix a pale salmon-pink color of stain (red, yellow, and white). Use this mixture to paint the nostrils, the tear ducts, the ear line, and the interior of the mouth. Apply a small amount of stain to the cheeks and gently spread it over the surface with a soft cotton cloth.

Coat the dry stain with sealer. When the first coat is dry, apply a second layer of sealer.

Setting the Eyes

The Goose Girl's eyes are oval, dark-brown, blown glass. The outside diameter of the pair used for the doll featured was 9/16 inch. Follow basically the same procedure for setting eyes in this bisque head as was used for setting them in composition heads. Refer to Chapter Seven (subsection: "Setting the Eyes") for a detailed description of this process.

You will need the following materials.

Materials

One pair of blown-glass eyes
Rubber cement
Sculpta Mold

Coat the inside of each eye socket with rubber cement. Place the glass eyes in the sockets. Position them carefully. Mix 1 tablespoon of Sculpta Mold with

½ tablespoon of water. Pack this material around the portion of the glass eyes inside the head. Press the eyes tightly into the sockets. Allow the compound several minutes to dry. Clean rubber cement off the surface of the eyes with a toothpick or similar tool.

12-3 Milvex composition body purchased from Seeley's Ceramic Service.

Assembling the Doll

As I mentioned earlier in this chapter, the head of the Goose Girl is attached to a ready-made composition body (fig. 12-3). If you ordered the body unassembled (unassembled bodies cost less), remove the pieces from the plastic bag and inspect each part for rough spots. Use fine sandpaper to gently smooth away these imperfections. The color is mixed with the composition. It is not a surface application so you need not be concerned about removing it with sanding. If you do not like the color of the body, repaint it with a premixed bisque stain or a mixture of your own. You can also use acrylic paints. Apply a coat of sealer or a coat of varnish (depending on the product you used) over the surface of all parts whether you left them alone or repainted them. When the first coat is dry, apply a second coat.

To string the pieces of the body together, you will need 2 feet of elastic cord and four 2-hole buttons ⅜ inch in diameter. To attach the swivel head to the body you will need a wooden thread spool (¾ inch in diameter) that has been sawed off, or a wooden neck button, or a ⅝-inch rubber stopper. You will also need a flexible wire such as nichrome or armature wire to bend into a hook, or a ready-made "S" hook. Wooden neck buttons, rubber neck stoppers, "S" hooks, and nichrome wire can be purchased from doll-parts suppliers.

To begin, cut two pieces of elastic cord 7½ inches in length. These are for the legs. Cut two pieces for the arms 4½ inches in length (if you are stringing a larger body, be sure to increase these measurements proportionately). Now, thread the end of an elastic leg cord in one button hole and out the other (fig. 12-4). Tie the cord in a secure knot. Use needle-nosed pliers to gently force the button into the hole in the lower portion of the composition leg. Once the button is inside, it should not slide back out of the hole when you pull on the elastic. If it does, use a larger button. Thread the ball-joint and then the upper leg over the elastic cord. Repeat this procedure and attach cord to the remaining leg and two arms. Next, place the elastic that extends from the legs inside the torso, through their respective sockets. Place the base of the legs in the sockets. Lay a stick across the neck socket. Bring the elastic leg cords up out of the body, through the neck opening. One should be on each side of the stick. Draw up the elastic, settling the legs firmly in their sockets. Knot the elastic in a secure knot. Follow this same procedure and place the arms in their sockets, knotting the arm elastic over the stick. Leave the knots on the stick and proceed to the next step.

Cut a piece of wire approximately 4½ inches in length. Double the wire and bend it into a hook (fig. 12-5). Punch the ends of the wire through the rubber stopper and bend them over its edges holding the hook in place. Use this same procedure when attaching the hook to a neck button or piece of thread spool, only in this case push the wire through the hole in the wood. Set the stopper, button, or spool in place inside the doll's head with the hook extending out the neck. Hook the wire under the knotted elastic leg and arm cords. Bend the wire hook closed with needle-nosed pliers, catching in the cord. Withdraw the stick and allow the elastic to settle back into the torso. It will draw the neck of the head tightly into its socket.

Next, plug the hole in the top of the head with a cork or a ready-made buckram skull crown. You will need a cork with a ⅞-inch diameter, and white glue. The cork should fit tightly in the hole. When it is correctly positioned, its upper surface will be level with the clay surface of the head. Trim the cork for a correct fit. Coat it with glue. Push it into position. When the glue is dry, the doll is assembled.

The Wig

The Goose Girl's wig is made of brown mohair yarn. It is gathered into "dusters" at the sides of her head and decorated with bows of bright pink embroidery thread. The mohair yarn is stitched to a fabric circle that is glued to her head. Refer to Chapter Six (subsection: "The Wig") for more information about mohair and wigmaking.

Materials

4 yards of mohair yarn
A fabric circle (matching the yarn color) 2½ inches
    in diameter
Thread to match the yarn
White glue

Cut the yarn into 7-inch strands. Run a line of basting stitches ⅛ inch within and around the perimeter of the fabric circle. Leave the ends of the thread dangling. Lay the fabric on a flat surface. Arrange half of the strands of yarn over the fabric circle (fig. 6-3). Stitch the yarn to the fabric, placing three equally spaced rows of stitching across its diameter. Arrange the remainder of the yarn over the fabric at right angles to the first. Stitch these strands to the fabric with three rows of stitching.

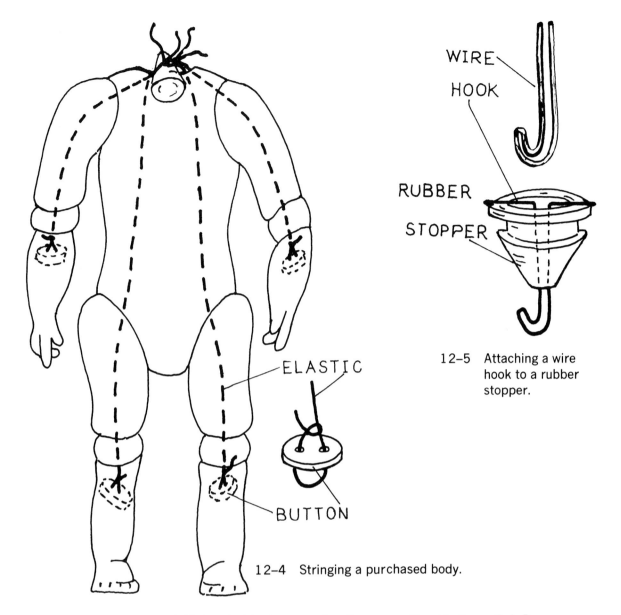

WIRE

HOOK

RUBBER

STOPPER

12–5 Attaching a wire hook to a rubber stopper.

ELASTIC

BUTTON

12–4 Stringing a purchased body.

Coat the doll's head with glue, covering the area outlined in figure 6-4. Draw up the basting stitches, slightly cupping the fabric circle. Press the cupped fabric over the glue. Hold the wig in place with rubber bands until the glue dries.

Trim the mohair that extends over the doll's face into short bangs. Part and divide the remainder of the strands into two dusters. Hold them in place with small rubber bands. Decorate the doll's hair with bows of bright embroidery thread.

The Clothing

The Goose Girl wears a long, peasant-style dress that has been cut from pink and blue calico printed cotton fabrics. The waist of the dress is decorated with a sash of pink satin ribbon. She also wears a white cotton half-slip, cotton panties, white knit ankle socks, and white felt shoes with blue embroidery-thread laces. A list of necessary materials follows.

12–6 The Goose Girl's clothing.

Materials

¼ yard of fabric for the dress skirt, sleeves, and collar
An 8 x 14-inch rectangle of compatible fabric for the bodice and ruffle of the dress
A 22-inch length of ¼-inch-wide satin ribbon
A rectangle of white cotton fabric 12 x 14 inches for the panties and slip
Two 6-inch lengths of ¼-inch-wide elastic and two 1¾-inch lengths for the sleeves
An 8 x 8-inch scrap of white knit fabric for the socks
2 tiny snap closures
A 5 x 5-inch piece of felt for the shoes
Two 7-inch strands of embroidery thread for shoe laces
Thread to match the fabrics

Use the patterns (figs. 12-7, 12-8) and cut the necessary number of pieces indicated from the fabric you have chosen. Cut a rectangle measuring 5 x 14 inches for the skirt of the dress. Cut three rectangles measuring 2 x 14 inches for the dress ruffle. Cut a rectangle measuring 5 x 14 inches for the slip. Transfer all markings to the wrong side of the fabrics.

THE PANTIES. Align the two pantie pieces and stitch one side seam from the base of the leg to the waist edge. Open out the piece. Press ½ inch of fabric along the waist edge to the inside. Stitch close to the raw edge of this folded piece, forming a casing for elastic (fig. 6-21). Thread a 6-inch length of elastic through the casing. Stitch the second side seam. Stitch the crotch seam. Hem the base of the legs. Press.

THE SLIP. Turn ½ inch of fabric to the inside along one long edge of the rectangle of slip fabric. Press. Stitch close to the raw edge of the folded piece, forming a casing for elastic. Thread a 6-inch length of elastic through the casing, stitching it to the ends of the casing. Stitch the short ends of the rectangle of slip fabric together from their base to the waist edge, stitching the ends of the casing together as you do so. Hem the lower edge of the slip. Press.

THE DRESS. Begin the dress by assembling the bodice. Stitch the bodice front to the bodice back pieces along the shoulder seams (7-14). Hem the back opening edges. Align the two collar pieces. Press ¼ inch of fabric along one notched edge to the inside (fig. 8-14). Stitch the unnotched edges of the collar pieces together. Turn the collar right side out. Press. With right sides together, align and baste the unfolded raw edge of the collar to the neck edge of the dress. Stitch. Press the seam toward the collar. By hand, stitch the folded edge of the collar over this seam.

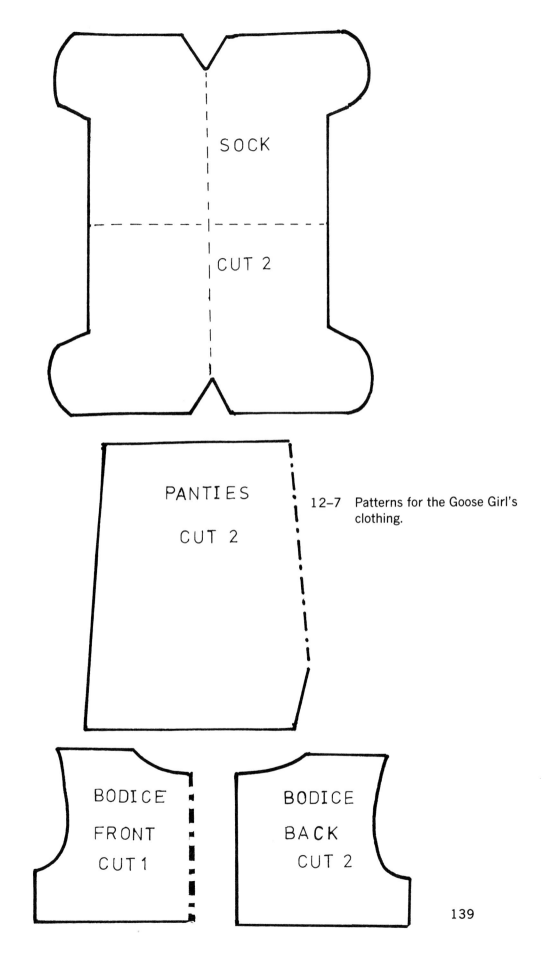

SOCK

CUT 2

PANTIES

CUT 2

12–7 Patterns for the Goose Girl's clothing.

BODICE
FRONT
CUT 1

BODICE
BACK
CUT 2

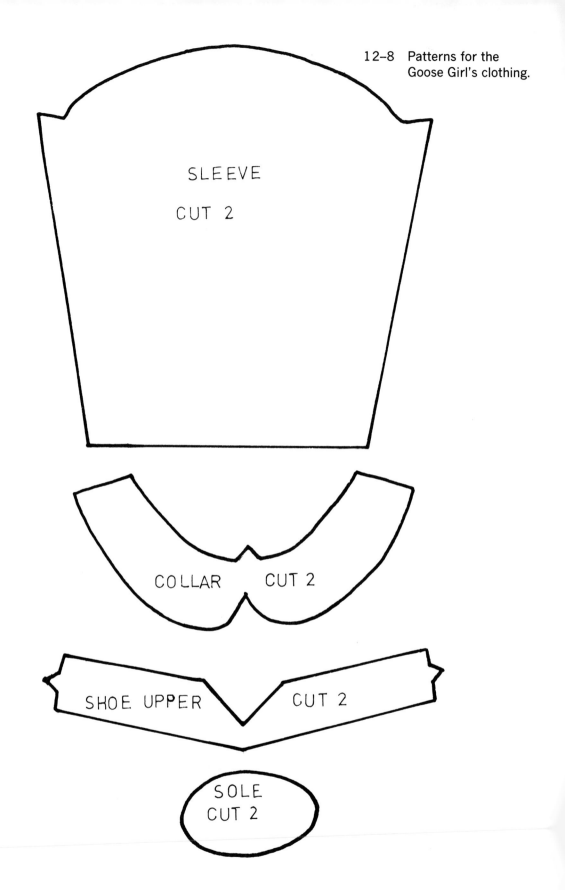

SLEEVE

CUT 2

COLLAR   CUT 2

SHOE UPPER   CUT 2

SOLE
CUT 2

To begin the sleeves, press ½ inch of fabric along the wrist end of each sleeve to the inside. Stitch close to the raw edge of each folded piece, forming a casing for elastic. Thread a 1¾-inch length of elastic through each casing. Stitch the pieces securely to the ends of the casings. Next, run a line of basting stitches ⅛ inch within the curved end of each sleeve. Draw up the stitching to slightly gather each sleeve. Align (right sides together) one sleeve with one armhole opening. Adjust the gathers so the sleeve fits the opening. Baste and then stitch the sleeve to the bodice (fig. 7-14). Repeat, attaching the second sleeve.

Stitch the underarm seam of the bodice from the wrist end of the sleeves to the waist of the bodice.

Before attaching the skirt to the bodice, attach the ruffle to the skirt. Stitch together the narrow ends of the three rectangular pieces of ruffle fabric, forming one long piece. Fold this piece in half, wrong sides together, forming a long narrow strip of fabric with two right sides (fig. 12-9). Press. Place a line of basting stitches ⅛ inch within the raw edge (opposite the fold) and the entire length of the piece. Draw up the stitching, gathering the piece to the length of the one side of the rectangle of skirt fabric (14 inches). Pin (with right sides together) the gathered strip to one long edge of the skirt (fig. 12-9). Stitch the ruffle to the skirt. Press the ruffle down.

Now, attach the skirt to the bodice. Begin by running a line of basting stitches along the edge of the skirt opposite the ruffle. Draw up these stitches, gathering the edge of the skirt to the length of the waist edge of the bodice. Pin the skirt to the bodice, overlapping the back edges of the bodice by ½ inch (fig. 8-15). Stitch the skirt to the bodice. Stitch the back of the skirt together, ending stitching 1 inch below the waist (fig. 10-19). Hem the raw edges.

Stitch two snap closures to the back opening edges of the bodice, placing one at the neck and one at the waist. Press. When the dress is on the doll, tie the sash of satin ribbon around her waist. Tack the ribbon in place with a few carefully concealed hand stitches.

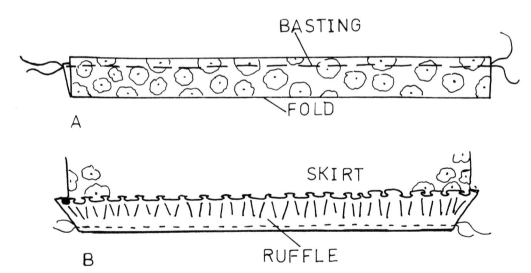

12-9 A. Folding and basting the ruffle.
      B. Stitching the ruffle to the base of the skirt.

SOCKS. Be sure the socks are cut from a fabric that stretches. To begin, fold one sock piece along the fold line marked on the fabric. You now have a double layer of fabric (fig. 8-12). Now fold the piece again so the toes are together, and you have four layers of fabric. Stitch from the top of the sock, down the front, around the toe, along the base of the foot, ending at the point where the fold begins. Turn the sock right side out. Turn ½ inch of fabric around the upper edge to the inside. Tack this edge to the seam with one or two stitches to hold it in place. Repeat and make the second sock.

THE SHOES. Use the sole pattern as a guide and cut two sole inserts from lightweight cadboard. Trim ¼ inch of cardboard from the perimeter of each piece. Glue a cardboard sole to each felt sole (fig. 8-13). Stitch the toe seam of the shoe uppers together, between the dots. Stitch the notched back edges of each piece together. Stitch a shoe upper to each sole (cardboard on the inside) using an overcast stitch. Lastly, stitch embroidery-thread drawstring laces around the upper edge of the shoes. Begin and end above the toe, leaving enough string dangling to tie in a bow. Stitch the thread in and out of the fabric. Place the shoes on the doll, over her socks. Draw up the stitching and tie the threads in a bow.

When she is dressed, the Goose Girl is complete.

SECTION III

CHAPTER 13
Porcelain

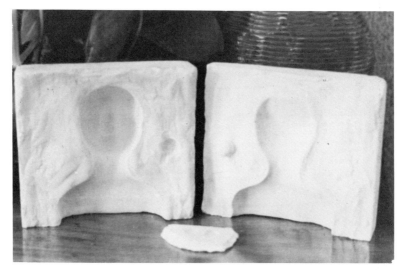

13–1   Plaster molds.

Porcelain is the undisputed monarch of mediums available to the dollmaker. This ceramic clay matures breathtakingly white and, to add to its beauty, is translucent. It has been the favorite clay of dollmakers for as long as they have possessed the technology to produce and use it.

Porcelain clay is said to have first been dug by the Chinese (as early as the sixth century) from a hill named Kao-ling. Kaolin, a refractory residual clay, is a main ingredient in porcelain bodies and takes its name from the hill of its original source. The Chinese kept porcelain a carefully guarded secret for centuries. When porcelain ware was finally exported, foreigners called it "china," a term that still denotes glazed porcelain.

An average porcelain body can be made by combining kaolin, ball clay, feldspar, and flint in almost equal quantities. Because kaolin is a residual clay, it fires beautifully white but is not plastic. Ball clay is added to increase plasticity (however, too much will also decrease whiteness). Feldspar is a flux that bonds the other materials together at high temperatures. It is the only flux needed for hard-paste porcelain. Soft-paste porcelain fires at lower temperatures and requires additional fluxes. Flint is a filler that is added to the porcelain body to make it less porous and to reduce warping. Hard-paste porcelains require very high firing temperatures, between cone 10 and cone 12. Soft-paste porcelain is more suited to the needs of the individual doll artist and can be fired at cone 6.

Today's doll artists have two options when it comes to using porcelain for making original dolls. Porcelain modeling clay can be purchased and one-of-a-kind originals hand modeled. Or a mold can be made from a prototype, and porcelain slip used to cast the doll parts. Both methods are discussed. Regardless of the method used to shape the doll, porcelain is fired to cone 6. The doll parts can then be china painted and are fired again, to cone 018.

MODELING

The techniques for modeling ceramic clay are explained in Chapter Nine. Read the section and use it as a guide for modeling porcelain clay doll parts. Follow the procedures for drying and firing outlined in the same chapter. However, if the clay that you purchased requires it, fire porcelain to cone 6 (2246° Fahrenheit) or higher. Cool. Polish the surface wtih fine sandpaper or a fine grit scrubber. Wear a protective face mask. Wash the polished porcelain with a mild dishwashing soap and water. Rinse well and dry before proceeding to china painting, which is discussed at the end of this chapter.

SLIP-CASTING PORCELAIN

To begin the procedure for slip-casting porcelain, it is necessary to design a doll and make a model of the design. A plaster mold is then made of this prototype, into which is poured the porcelain slip. The plaster quickly absorbs the moisture from the slip, causing the clay to harden sufficiently in a matter of minutes to hold its shape. The doll part is then removed from the mold and the drying process is continued until the pieces are bone dry. They are then fired to cone 6.

Chapter Five contains much information on mold-making. Read the subsection entitled "Making a Plaster Mold for Composition." Many of the procedures explained in that section will be employed during the process of slip-casting porcelain.

The following steps guide the dollmaker toward the production of a two-piece square or rectangular mold. Molds that require more than two pieces are briefly discussed after this section.

STEP 1: *Designing the Prototype.* Do a series of drawings or make a rough clay model of the doll you plan to produce. Decide now, if you are making a shoulder-plate head and lower limbs or a swivel head. Remember that a plaster mold will be made from this design. Avoid undercuts.

STEP 2: *Modeling.* The model from which the mold is made can be constructed of either oil-base (plastiline) or water-base (white talc or porcelain) clay. Model an accurate, symmetrical, and sturdy reproduction of your design. When you are satisfied with the structure, smooth the surface. A finger dipped in water will smooth plastiline. Use a damp cloth or a wooden modeling tool to smooth the surface of water clay.

If you plan to use set-in eyes, or if it is a swivel head, slice off the top of the model's head (fig. 9-3). If you have constructed lower limbs that are to be attached to a fabric body, build a lip and groove at the base of each (fig. 10-4). If you are making the entire body, provide a system for stringing elastic cord from limb to limb (fig. 8-7). Last, if this is a first mold, model the ears separately from the head.

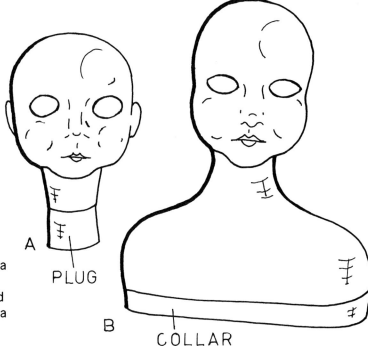

13-2 A. Plug attached to the base of a swivel head.
      B. Collar attached to the base of a shoulder-plate head.

A

PLUG

B

COLLAR

Model and attach a clay plug or collar (fig. 13-2) extending from the base of each model. This clay addition will provide each mold with a channel into which to pour slip.

A prototype constructed of water clay should be allowed to become leather-hard. When it reaches this stage, store it in a plastic bag to prevent its becoming bone dry. It is not necessary to hollow out or fire this model. Plastiline prototypes are ready to use as soon as the modeling is completed.

You can make a mold of a fired head, though this is a risky process. If the fired head produces a mold with undercuts you are in danger of breaking both the head and the mold when you try to open the mold.

STEP 3: *Bedding.* To determine mold seams, inspect the model and decide where the widest points are. The line of division must cut across the center of these points, dividing the model into two parts. Lightly and accurately etch this line into the surface of the clay (see Chapter Five).

Lay the clay model on a flat surface positioned exactly as it will be in the mold. Build a wall of clay from the work surface up to the line of division. The wall should be solid and level, extending several inches beyond and surrounding the prototype (fig. 13-5). Do not cover the base of the plug or collar. This procedure is called bedding. Bed a model constructed of oil-base clay in water clay. A water-clay model should be bedded in oil clay. Oil clay will not adhere to water clay, and vice versa. Or you can coat a water-clay model with vaseline and then bed it in water clay. A fired head should be coated with ceramic sealer and, after this application is dry, vaseline. It can be bedded in either oil- or water-base clay.

Trim the outside edges of the clay bed. They should be straight (fig. 13-5). If the edges of the bed are left uneven, the mold boards will not fit tightly.

You can make a single mold that will cast more than one piece. This works well if the models are generally the same size (for example, a set of lower limbs). Lay the pieces in a row on a flat surface positioned as they will be in the mold. The base of the clay plugs must be even (fig. 15-3). Combine the pieces within one clay bed.

STEP 4: *Retaining Walls.* Retaining walls surround the prototype and hold the liquid plaster in place until it hardens. Mold boards, which produce square or rectangular molds, are the traditional method employed. An alternate method, which can be substituted, will produce a round mold. Bed the model in clay (do not square off the edges of the bed) and place it in a plastic bowl. The sides of the bowl serve as retaining walls. Instructions follow for building a set of mold boards capable of making a square mold as large as 14 square inches and which can be adjusted to produce square or rectangular molds of various smaller sizes. You will need the following materials.

Materials

4 smooth wooden boards that measure (actual size)
    ¾ inch x 5½ inches x 16 inches
4 pieces of wood that measure (actual size) ⅝ inch x
    1 inch x 5½ inches
12 nails or 12 flat-head screws 1¼ inch in length
    with ¼-inch heads
Four 2½-inch or 3-inch C-clamps

Boards with a formica surface can be used, but smooth boards, well sized with mold soap, work just as well. Nail or screw one strip of wood over the end, aligning it with the edge of each board (fig. 13-3). The strip creates a lip for joining the boards at right angles to one another. The boards are held in place with the clamps (fig. 13-4).

Place your model on a work surface that can easily be cleaned. Plaster will be poured inside the mold boards. Plaster is always messy! Tightly surround

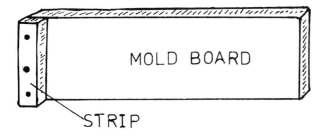

MOLD BOARD

STRIP

13–3 Attaching strip to mold board.

13–4 Mold boards.

the clay bed with the mold boards (fig. 13-5). Adjust the C-clamps so the boards are permanently positioned against the clay. Pack more clay around the outside base of the boards and up each side of the joints between boards. This additional precaution will help prevent plaster seeping out tiny cracks.

Apply soap size to the portion of the mold boards extending above the clay bed (see Chapter Five). If your prototype is water clay, coat its exposed surface with a thin, smooth application of vaseline. A fired head should also be coated with vaseline. Plastiline or damp water clay will not bond with the plaster.

STEP 6: *The Mold.* Follow the basic directions for mixing plaster presented in Chapter Five. However, do not wait until the plaster is thickened to the "cheese" state. Pour the plaster into the mold while it is still liquid. It should be poured just after it begins to coat the stirring utensil, when it is the consistency of heavy cream. Another cue: When the stirring stick leaves a slight impression after being dragged across the surface, the plaster is ready to pour.

Pour the plaster quickly and evenly inside the mold boards. The plaster should be poured against the clay bed, not onto the surface of the model. As the plaster increases in depth, it will flow over the piece. This procedure helps eliminate air bubbles, which might otherwise be trapped against the surface of the model. Continue pouring plaster until it is at least 1 inch deep over the highest point on the model. When you have finished pouring, jar the work surface two or three times to dispel air bubbles.

Allow the plaster time to set up. This wil take thirty to forty minutes. As soon as it starts to cool, the plaster is hard.

Remove the mold boards that surround the hardened plaster. Reverse the model. The plaster will be on the bottom with the clay bed on top. Remove the

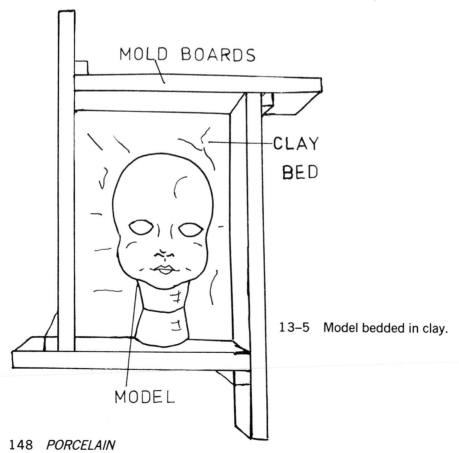

MOLD BOARDS

CLAY

BED

13–5 Model bedded in clay.

MODEL

clay from around the model. Do not remove the model from the mold. Carefully clean the surface of the plaster, removing any remaining clay particles.

Make mold keys (see Chapter Five).

Size the plaster surface of the mold that will come in contact with the second pouring of plaster. Resize the mold boards. Coat the surface of water clay or fired models with vaseline.

Place mold boards around the plaster and tightly fix them in place with clamps. Again pack clay around the base and joints of the boards to prevent plaster leaks.

If you modeled the ears separately, size the interior of a small cardboard jewelry box with mold soap. Place the ears inside, on the floor of the box. When you pour the second half of the mold, pour plaster into this box, covering the ear models, creating an ear mold.

Mix a second batch of plaster. Pour the second half of the mold. Allow the plaster to set up. This section of the mold will take longer to cool than the first. When the plaster is hard, remove the boards.

Gently open the mold. Occasionally it is necessary to place an implement, such as a screw driver, against the mold seam and tap it with a hammer to jar the pieces apart.

If the model slides easily out of the mold everything is as it should be. If the model scrapes or tears when you try to remove it, undercuts are present. Minor problems can be solved by sanding the interior of the plaster mold. If the problem is major, model a corrected prototype and repour the problem half of the mold.

Use extrafine sandpaper or a fine grit scrubber to smooth areas of the casting surface of the mold that require this treatment. Take care—plaster can be easily scratched.

Dry the mold, closed and banded wtih large rubber bands (Chapter Five). This process will take several days, depending on humidity and the procedure you follow.

STEP 7: *Pouring Porcelain Slip.* Slip is liquid water-base clay that has been deflocculated. Clay is made up of tiny platelike particles called flocs. These flocs have a great attraction for one another. The fact that they cling together, yet slide over one another, makes clay plastic. To turn clay into slip, deflocculation is achieved by adding a small amount of water plus an alkaline substance such as liquid silicate of soda. The alkaline substance breaks the attraction that the clay particles have for one another, suspending them evenly throughout the water.

Newly made slip is aged for several days before it is used.

Porcelain slip can be purchased in gallon containers. Doll-parts suppliers offer slip specially formulated to turn flesh color when the castings are fired. Coloring agents can be purchased separately and mixed with white slip if you prefer an alternate color. A list of suppliers can be found after the text.

Slip must be thoroughly stirred before it is poured. Unstirred slip produces castings with rings of different colors. A dowel stick with a ½-inch diameter makes a good stirring tool. Like plaster, slip should not be beaten. Beating induces air bubbles to form in the mixture. Simply stir the mixture gently back and forth. When the slip is of an even consistency and color throughout the mixture, it is ready to pour.

Slip that is too thick is difficult to pour. Thinning slip with water may ruin it. If you have no alternative, add a drop or two at a time, stirring after each addition. A better method to employ when thinning slip is to mix 1 teaspoon of powdered sodium silicate with ½ cup of hot water. Add this solution, 1 teaspoonful at a time to 1 gallon of slip. Stir as you make each addition. Continue

13–6 Stirring slip.

until the correct consistency has been attained. Sodium silicate can be purchased from ceramic supply houses.

High humidity and cold adversely affect slip casting. Ideally, slip should be at least seventy degrees to be the correct consistency when poured. Humidity affects the mold. Plaster is less likely to absorb moisture if the humidity is too high. The casting may not set up. Consider these facts before filling the mold.

It is important to pour slip into the mold in a uniform, continuous stream. Any pauses will result in ridges on the surface of the doll parts. A vessel with a narrow, round spout makes pouring easier. A clean, disposable, ½-gallon plastic container, like those that hold orange juice, cider, or other drinks, works well (fig. 13-7). Be sure you have sufficient slip in the container to fill the mold before beginning to pour.

Now, carefully clean your mold. It should be free of foreign particles. These will bond with the slip and show up on the surface of the doll part, contaminating the piece.

Band the mold tightly closed with heavy rubber bands (available at ceramic supply houses) and set the mold on a level surface that has been protected with newspapers. The channel, into which the slip is poured, must be on the top side.

13–7 Containing for pouring slip.

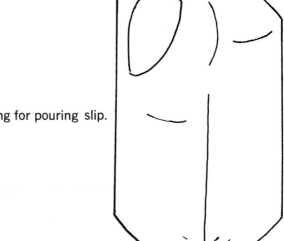

13–8   Draining mold.

Pour slip into the mold. Do not hesitate, but do not rush either. Slow and steady is the key to success. Try to guide the stream of slip so it flows into the mold against one wall of the channel. This will keep pinholes, caused by air bubbles, to a minimum. Fill the mold to the top of the channel.

As soon as the slip comes in contact with the plaster, the plaster begins to absorb the moisture in the slip. The level of the slip will drop, and it is necessary to add more slip to the mold. Keep it well above the point where the pouring channel connects with the doll part. This is called "topping off."

After three to five minutes, cut a notch in the waste section (pouring channel) of the casting to check the thickness of the walls. Continue to check every couple of minutes until the walls are the correct thickness for the size of the piece you have poured. Then, pour the excess slip back into the gallon container. Do not turn the mold upside down and let the slip rush out. This may cause a vacuum which will pull the sides of the casting into the hollow center of the mold. Instead, tip the mold at an angle and gently pour the excess slip into the container. This method allows air to enter as the slip leaves the mold.

Prop the mold, slightly angled, over the slip container and let it drain for a few additional minutes. (fig. 13-8). The angle prevents drips from dropping from the top of the interior of the mold onto the cast surface below. Drips will form bumps on the outside wall of the finished piece. When all obvious drain-

13–9   Mold supported on wooden slats for additional draining.

ing has ceased, set the mold, raised above the work surface (again slightly angled) on 1 x 2-inch wooden slats (fig. 13-9). The slats recommended for drying ceramic pieces are suitable.

Allow the casting to be set up. A piece that is set up is damp, yet firm. It can be removed from the mold intact. There are several variables affecting the amount of time this process will take. The moisture content of the mold as well as that of the slip affects setting up.

The casting should be ready to remove from the mold within an hour. Generally the visible surface of the clay will appear dull, not shiny, when it is sufficiently dry.

Try to open the mold. If it does not open easily, be patient. Rather than force it open, set it near a source of heat such as an oven or heat vent. Several minutes of warming will usually release the casting.

If a casting sticks to the mold in spots, it is probably a new mold that has not dried sufficiently or a mold that has not been dried between castings. The mold, in other words, is water-soaked and must be redried. A mold must be dried after each casting.

Before lifting the damp, fragile casting from the mold, remove all jewelry from your fingers. The surface of the casting can be easily indented. Cup your hands, cradling the piece with your palms, after you draw it from the mold.

Inspect the clay. If tiny holes (caused by air bubbles) are present, smooth them closed with the water-dampened bristles of a soft brush.

Remove separately cast ears from their mold. With slip, coat the inside surface of the ear and the surface of the head where the ear will be positioned. Place the ear on the head. Gently, using a modeling tool, blend the edges of the ear into the clay of the head.

STEP 8: *Fettling.* Fettling is a trimming procedure. This should be done soon after the doll part is removed from the mold. Cut eye sockets, punch holes, and shape shoulder plates, cut the hole in the top of the head, and trim away mold seams or rough areas. Proceed carefully and patiently—the piece is fragile.

Save any pieces of clay fettled from the casting. Also save any unfired, warped, or broken pieces. Store the scraps in a plastic bag. They can be reclaimed. When you have collected a sufficient quantity, add water to the bag. Seal the bag tightly and let it sit overnight. The clay will absorb the water. Knead it, and you will have porcelain modeling clay.

STEP 9: *Drying.* The plaster has absorbed a large portion of the water of plasticity from the clay. It will be leather-hard in one day and bone dry in two or three days. During drying and firing, porcelain slip-cast pieces shrink, just as do modeling clays. The finished piece will be 18 to 20 percent smaller than the damp casting.

When the piece is leather-hard, gently smooth the surface of the casting with a piece of nylon stocking. Also, sand the inside of the eye sockets so the eyes will fit tightly. Wrap the eraser end of a pencil with fine sandpaper. It makes a handy tool for accomplishing this chore.

Allow the piece to become bone dry.

STEP 10: *Firing.* Fire the bone-dry doll parts to cone 6 (2246° Fahrenheit). Follow the general procedures for firing doll parts as outlined in Chapter Nine.

STEP 11: *Polishing.* Polish the cool, fired pieces with fine sandpaper or a fine grit scrubber. Wear a protective face mask to prevent inhalation of dust or grit. Use mild soap and water to wash the surface clean, removing any impurities that might contaminate the china paint. The piece should be thoroughly dry before you begin china painting. If you use a drying cloth, be sure it is lint free.

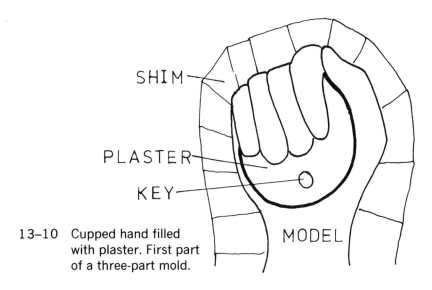

SHIM

PLASTER

KEY

MODEL

13-10 Cupped hand filled
with plaster. First part
of a three-part mold.

MOLDS WITH MORE THAN TWO PARTS

Two-part molds are less complicated than those with more parts; however, they encourage stylization and demand simplicity of the doll design. Occasionally a dollmaker may wish to produce a more intricate doll. One way to solve this problem would be to make more than one two-piece mold and assemble the doll after casting. The molding of separate ears in the last section was a simple illustration of this method. Another solution to the moldmaking problems presented by intricacy is to make a mold with more than two pieces.

A hand with the fingers closed over the palm would require a three-piece mold. If you attempted to pour a two-piece mold, plaster would pour into the palm and become trapped under the fingers, creating an undercut. To make a three-part mold of the hand, first fill the palm with plaster (fig. 13-10) to the level of the fingers. When the plaster in the palm has set up, make a notch or key in the plaster surface so the other parts of the mold will hold it in place. Coat it with size. With the plaster piece in place in the hand, divide the arm as you would for a two-piece mold. Bed the piece in clay. Set the mold boards and pour a traditional two-piece mold.

This procedure becomes more involved when dividing a head with modeled curls for a mold of several parts, but the theory is the same. Keep in mind that each piece of the mold should cover as large an area of the model as possible without creating undercuts.

REDUCING A HEAD

Dollmakers who are interested in making dollhouse dolls often prefer to model a large original head and reduce it. It is easier to model detail on a large head than on a tiny one. Reducing is a simple procedure that uses the natural shrinkage of clay during drying and firing to this advantage.

Make a mold of the head that is to be reduced. Cast three or four heads. Dry and fire each. They will now be four-fifths the size of the original head. Pick the best fired head. Coat it with vaseline and make a second mold. Again, cast,

13–11 China painting.

dry, and fire three or four heads. These heads will be smaller than the first group. Make a third mold, continuing the procedure until you have a head of the correct size.

FINISHING THE PORCELAIN SURFACE—CHINA PAINTING

China painting is an ancient art that the dollmaker may wish to assimilate into his/her repertoire to produce porcelain dolls with lustrous faces.

Generally, china painting involves suspending a pigment in an oil and then applying the mixture to a fired porcelain surface. The piece is then refired to cone 018. This burns off the oil while softening the surface of the porcelain so it may absorb the china colors. The colors become permanent, and the only way to remove them after firing is to fire the piece again, to a high temperature (cone 6), and burn them off.

China colors can be purchased moist or dry and with a flat or gloss finish. The finish is a matter of taste. Moist colors are convenient, but dry colors last longer and are more economical. To begin, purchase the following colors: pompadour red, flesh red, yellow, yellow-brown, blue, black, and white.

You will also need a piece of heavy glass or a tile to use as a palate on which to mix pigments with oil. A palate knife makes the best mixing tool.

The dry pigments are suspended in a painting medium that can be purchased premixed, or you can mix your own. Two recipes follow.

Recipe I

Place a shallow, broad-based dish of gummed turpentine in direct sunlight. Allow it to evaporate until it becomes an oil.

Recipe II

1 cup of copaiba balsam (oleo resin obtained from
    South American tree)
½ tablespoon of lavender oil
¼ tablespoon oil of cloves

The above ingredients can be ordered from drug stores. Thin Recipe II with

154 *PORCELAIN*

a drop of oil of cloves and thicken it by adding more copaiba balsam. Ideally, it should be the consistency of thin honey.

To make dry colors moist, place a pea-sized pile of dry pigment on the palate. Add one drop of painting medium. Mix, using the palate knife to grind (in a circular motion) the grains of paint against the palate. Add more medium if necessary. The paint should be thick, like honey, and smooth, without graininess. If the paint is too grainy, a flux can be added during mixing. Flux is a white powder that helps fuse the colors to the porcelain.

In addition to a china-painting medium, a pen medium can be used. Pure anise oil is an excellent pen medium. One drop added to any mixed color will turn the paint into ink. To produce fine, hard lines, use crow-quill pens and fine points.

China painting requires good quality brushes. The paints are spoiled when contaminated by lint, dust, or straying brush hairs. To start your brush collection, purchase a 6/0 round red sable for tiny soft lash lines. A 3/0 round red sable is good for slightly larger areas of detail. A number 6 stippler aids in the application of cheek color (fig. 5-13).

Gently wash new brushes in mild soap and water to remove loose hairs. Allow them to dry. Condition the brushes by immersing them in painting medium for twenty minutes. Before beginning work, remove all excess medium on a piece of lint-free cloth. Clean the brushes with gum turpentine. Gently swish them through the cleaning fluid. Never stab the bristles against the bottom of the container. The bristles will break.

China paints are applied in successive layers. The work is fired between layers. The colors are developed by degrees, from light to dark. Some colors—reds, for instance—burn off. Paint these areas slightly darker than the color anticipated after firing.

A lint-free cloth, dampened with painting medium, can be used to remove incorrectly applied paint.

China paints are fired to cone 018 (1328° Fahrenheit). Be sure your kiln is clean. Vacuum before each firing of painted doll parts. Remove dust and grit from elements, grooves, floor shelves, and the top of the kiln. Do not use hydrated alumina on the shelves. Fire the stacked pieces in a bare kiln.

Leave the kiln door cracked for the first thirty minutes of the firing cycle. This allows the oil to burn off. There will be an odor. Close the door and fire to cone 018. As soon as this temperature is reached, turn off the kiln. Allow it to cool.

When the kiln is cool and you have removed your work, inspect the color. If it is too dark, fire the piece to cone 6 and burn off the color. If it is too light, repaint, using the same colors and fire again to cone 018.

If the paint peels or flakes off the porcelain after firing, the paint was applied too heavily. Mix more painting medium with the pigments and apply thinner coats of paint.

If the colors fade, it indicates that too much painting medium was used to the ratio of pigment.

A painted surface that feels grainy after it has been removed from the kiln has been contaminated with the kiln dust. Smooth the surface with a fine grit scrubber. Clean the kiln.

Specks of color on a piece may indicate that a heavy application of paint on a piece fired at an earlier date melted and splattered on the walls and elements of the kiln. Reheating the kiln caused the paint to remelt and splatter, contaminating the new piece. Gently sand the paint off the fire brick. Vacuum the kiln.

The two following chapters contain projects that further explore the use of porcelain and china paints to produce dolls.

CHAPTER 14
Project Seven-Rapunzel

14-1 Rapunzel.

Rapunzel was the most beautiful child under the sun. She had splendid long hair, as fine as spun gold. Her plaits fell twenty ells downwards.

The Brothers Grimm

Rapunzel has a modeled porcelain head. Her features are china painted, except her eyes, which are blue blown glass. Her wig is made of golden-yellow mohair yarn. Her swivel head is attached to a ready-made composition body. She wears a pale blue and white printed dress. The dress is covered by a lacy pinafore. Her undergarments include a half-slip and pantalets. She wears white felt shoes.

The doll is 9½ inches tall. The circumference of her head is 7 inches.

Modeling

Rapunzel's head is modeled of reclaimed flesh-colored porcelain scraps. Porcelain scraps from fettling or breakage are collected, remoisturized, and kneaded. The result is modeling clay. This procedure is explained more thoroughly in Chapter Thirteen (subsection: "Fettling"). If you have not done so, read Chapter Nine to familiarize yourself with modeling, drying, and firing procedures.

A list of materials necessary to make one 7-inch swivel head follows.

Materials

A 1-pound lump of wedged, flesh-colored porcelain
    modeling clay
China paints

Take into consideration the approximate 20-percent shrinkage of the clay, and model a swivel head that will be proportionately correct and can be attached to a 7-inch body. The base of the neck should have a diameter of 1¼ inches before drying and firing. Refer to the photograph (fig. 14-2) and use it as a guide when modeling.

When satisfied with the structure and modeling of the head, smooth the surface of the clay. Then, begin the drying process.

Hollow out the head when it is leather-hard. The walls should be uniform and no thicker than ½ inch. Cut a hole 1 inch in diameter in the top of the head (fig. 7-5). Cut out eye sockets following the procedure outlined in Chapter Seven. Make them larger than the projected sockets, taking shrinkage into account. Use a sharp feather knife (fig. 11-3A).

Place the head, raised above the work surface, on wooden slats. Drape a piece of damp cotton sheeting over the piece. Control the drying process. The head should be bone dry in seven to ten days.

Fire the head, placed on a bed of hydrated alumina, to cone 6 (2246° Fahrenheit). Cool.

14–2 Rapunzel's head.

Polish the fired head to a satiny smoothness. Use fine sandpaper or a fine grit scrubber. Wear a face mask. Wash the head with mild soap and water to remove dust. When the head is dry it can be china painted.

China Painting

Read Chapter Thirteen (subsection: "Finishing the Porcelain Surface—China Painting") if you have not done so.

The head is flesh-colored already, so begin by painting the light-colored areas of the features. Coat the cheeks with a thin application of painting medium. Dab a small spot of pompadour red onto the center of each cheek. Spread the color over the cheek. Paint the lips, nostrils, and ear lines with this color.

Fire the doll to 018 to set this application of color. Cool.

Paint the nostrils, eyebrows, tear ducts, and lashes (that rim the upper half of the eye socket) with yellow-brown paint darkened slightly by the addition of a dab of black. Also, line the inside of the eye sockets and outline the lips with this color. If you prefer, use a pen and draw the lashes and brows and outline the mouth. A pen produces a more uniform but, also, a harder line.

Once more, fire the head to cone 018. Cool.

Setting the Eyes

Rapunzel's eyes are oval blue blown glass and have an outside diameter of 9/16 inch. They are set following the same procedures used for the Snow Queen's eyes. For additional information on this procedure read Chapter Seven (subsection: "Setting the Eyes").

If you prefer, molds can be purchased for slip-casting porcelain eyes. The fired eyes can be glazed, china painted, or bisque stained. They are very effective.

Materials

A matching pair of blown-glass eyes
Rubber cement
Sculpta Mold

Drop the eyes into the sockets to see if they fit. You may find it necessary to substitute a size of eye, larger or smaller, depending on shrinkage during drying and firing. Coat the inside of the eye sockets with rubber cement. Press the glass eyes into place. Carefully position them. Mix 1 tablespoon of Sculpta Mold with ½ tablespoon of water. Pack this modeling compound around the portion of the eyes inside the head. Push the eyes tightly against the clay. The Sculpta Mold will be dry in a few minutes. Clean rubber cement off the surface of the eye with a toothpick or similar tool.

Assembling the Body

Rapunzel's head is attached to a 7-inch German ball-jointed, Milvex composition body that was purchased from Seeley's Ceramic Service, Inc., of Oneonta, New York (see Sources of Supply). This is the same type of body to which the head of the Goose Girl (fig. 12-3) is attached. Follow the instructions outlined in Chapter Twelve (subsection: "Assembling the Doll") for stringing together the limbs and attaching the swivel head.

Materials

Ceramic sealer
2½ feet of elastic cord
Four buttons with 2 holes and a ½-inch diameter
A ⅝-inch rubber stopper or wooden neck button
A 5½-inch length of ¹⁄₁₆-inch wire or a ready-made
    "S" hook
A cork with a 1-inch diameter or a ready-made
    buckram skull crown
White glue

The Wig

Rapunzel's wig is composed of mohair yarn. To produce her long braids you will need 23 yards of golden-yellow yarn. If you are not already familiar with the process, read the background information in Chapter Six (subsection: "The Wig").

Materials

23 yards of mohair yarn
A fabric circle with a circumference of 2½ inches
    that is close to the color of the yarn
Thread to match the yarn

To begin, cut the yarn into 28 strands, each 29 inches in length. Then, run a basting stitch ⅛ inch within and around the perimeter of the fabric circle. Leave the ends of the thread dangling. Lay the fabric on a flat surface. Arrange half of the strands of yarn across the circle (fig. 6-3). Stitch the yarn in place with three rows of stitching. Arrange the remainder of the yarn over the fabric at right angles to the first strands. Stitch it in place. Coat the doll's head with white glue, roughly covering the area outlined in figure 6-4. Draw up the basting stitches, slightly gathering the fabric into a cup. Press the cupped fabric over the glue. Hold the wig in place with rubber bands until the glue dries.

When the glue is dry, style the hair by parting the yarn down the center of the head and plaiting it into two braids. Hold the braids in place with small rubber bands. A circle of decorative trim featuring embroidered flowers is stitched to the wig, encircling Rapunzel's head.

The Clothing

Rapunzel's dress is cotton. The ends of the sleeves are decorated with gathered lace edging. The neckline is bound with satin ribbon. Her pinafore is cotton-lace fabric. It is also decorated with gathered lace edging and one embroidered flower. Her undergarments are white cotton. Her shoes are white felt. The following materials are necessary to make her clothing.

Materials

¼ yard of fabric for the dress
¼ yard of fabric for the pinafore
¼ yard of fabric for the slip and pantalets
A 5 x 9-inch rectangle of felt for the shoes
A 26-inch length of ½-inch-wide gathered lace
    edging
Two 5½-inch lengths of ¼-inch-wide elastic
4 tiny snap closures
Two 7-inch lengths of embroidery thread for
    shoelaces
A 5-inch length of ¼-inch-wide satin ribbon to bind

Use the patterns (figs. 14-3, 14-4) as guides and cut the number of pieces indicated on the patterns from the fabrics you have chosen. Also, cut a rectangle of fabric measuring 6½ x 15 inches for the skirt of the dress. Cut a rectangle of lace fabric measuring 5 x 18 inches for the skirt of the pinafore. Cut a rectangle of white cotton fabric measuring 5½ x 16 inches for the slip. Transfer markings to the wrong side of the fabrics.

THE PANTALETS. Stitch together one side seam of the pair of pantalet pieces from the base of the leg to the waist edge (fig. 7-13). Press the piece open and flat. Turn ½ inch of fabric along the waist edge to the inside. Press this turned edge in place. Stitch close to the raw edge of the piece, forming a casing for elastic (fig. 6-21). Thread a 5½-inch length of elastic through the casing. Stitch the piece securely to both ends of the casing. Stitch the second side seam. Stitch the crotch seam. Hem the base of the legs.

THE SLIP. Following the above procedure, make a casing for elastic on one long edge of the rectangle of slip fabric (fig. 6-21). Thread a 5½-inch length of elastic through the casing and stitch it securely to both ends. Stitch together the narrow ends of the slip fabric. Hem the base. Press the slip.

THE DRESS. Stitch the front bodice to the two back-bodice pieces, along the shoulder seams (fig. 7-14). Hem the back opening edges. With the right side of the ribbon against the wrong side of the neck edge, stitch the pair together. Place the line of stitching 1/16 of an inch within the edge of each (fig. 14-5). Fold the ribbon over the seam to the outside of the dress. The wrong side of the ribbon and the right side of the dress will be together. Press. Stitch close to the edge of the ribbon, stitching it to the neckline of the dress. Hem the raw ends of the ribbon.

Turn, press, and stitch ¼ inch of fabric along the wrist end of each sleeve to the inside. Cut a piece of gathered lace edging the length of this hem. Stitch the lace over the hem. Then, run a line of basting stitches ⅛ inch within the curved end of each sleeve. Draw up this stitching, slightly gathering the sleeves. Align the gathered edge with the armhole of the bodice. Adjust the gathers so the sleeve fits the armhole. Baste and then stitch a sleeve to each armhole.

Stitch the underarm seams, stitching together the ends of the lace as you do so.

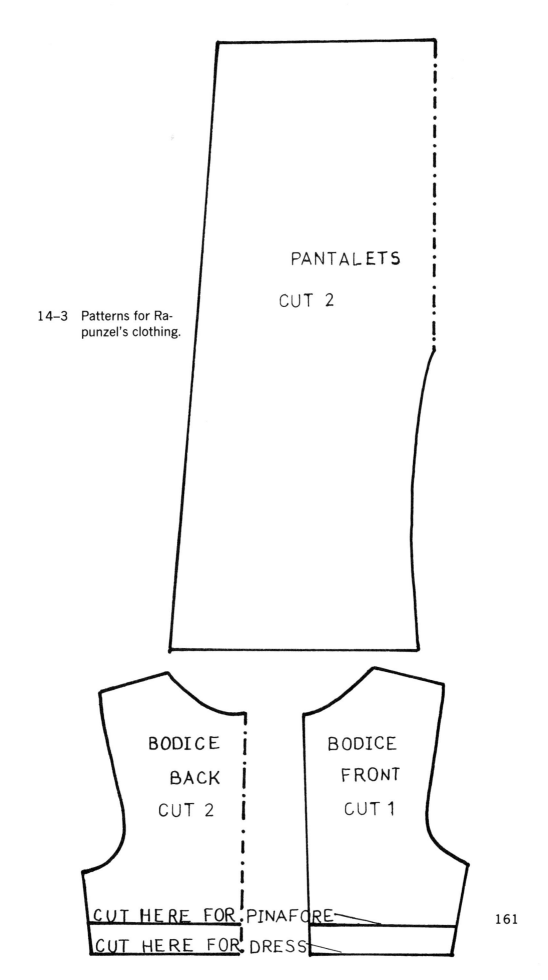

PANTALETS

CUT 2

14–3 Patterns for Ra-
punzel's clothing.

BODICE

BACK

CUT 2

BODICE

FRONT

CUT 1

CUT HERE FOR PINAFORE

CUT HERE FOR DRESS

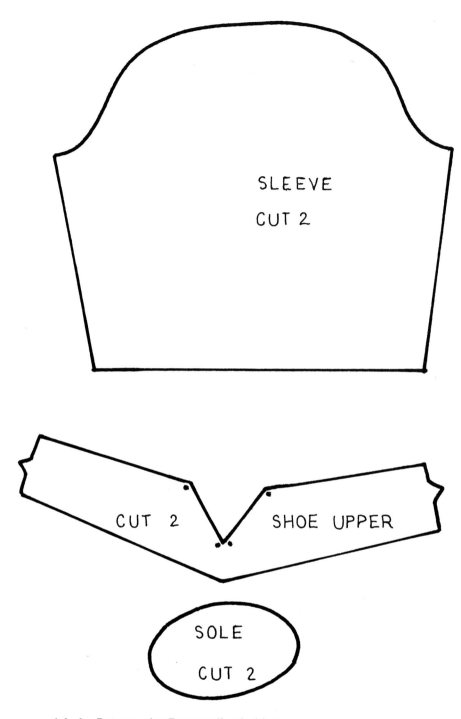

SLEEVE

CUT 2

CUT 2   SHOE UPPER

SOLE

CUT 2

14–4   Patterns for Rapunzel's clothing.

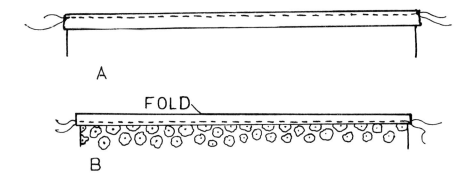

A

FOLD

B

14-5 A. Stitching ribbon to inside of fabric edge.
       B. Folding ribbon over the edge and stitching it to the right side
         of the fabric.

To attach the skirt to the bodice, place a line of basting ⅛ inch within the one long edge of the rectangle of skirt fabric. Draw up this stitching to gather the edge to the length of the waist edge of the bodice. Pin the skirt to the right side of the bodice (fig. 8-15). The skirt should overlap the back opening edges of the bodice by ½ inch. Stitch the skirt to the bodice. Stitch the back of the skirt together, ending stitching 1-inch below the waist of the bodice (fig. 10-19). Hem these raw edges. Hem the base of the skirt.

Stitch two tiny snap closures to the back opening edges of the bodice. Place one at the neck and one at the waist. Press the finished dress.

THE PINAFORE. Stitch the front of the bodice to the back pieces along the shoulder seams. Stitch the underarm seams. Hem the neck edge, the back opening edges, and the armhole openings.

Follow the same procedure and attach the skirt to the slip as you attached the skirt to the dress. Do not stitch the back of the skirt together. Hem the back edges and hem the base of the skirt. Stitch a piece of gathered lace edging over the hem of the skirt. Turn the ends of the lace to the inside of the back opening edges. Stitch them in place.

Stitch two tiny snap closures to the neck and waist of the back opening edges of the bodice. Stitch one brightly colored embroidered flower to the front of the bodice. Press the pinafore. Use a warm iron on lace fabric. It is easily scorched.

THE SHOES. Use the sole pattern as a guide and cut two soles of light-weight cardboard. Glue a cardboard sole to each felt sole. The cardboard insert should be on the inside of the shoe. Use white glue or liquid latex as the adhesive. Stitch together the toe seam between the dots marked on each felt upper. Stitch the heel seam of each. Turn the uppers right side out. By hand, using an overcast stitch, stitch a felt upper to each sole (fig. 8-13). Stitch embroidery-thread laces encircling the upper edge of each shoe. Begin above the toe and stitch the thread in and out of the fabric, ending stitching above the toe. Draw up the stitching and tie the threads in a bow.

Dress Rapunzel and Project Seven is complete.

CHAPTER 15
Project Eight-The Mermaid

15–1   The Mermaid.

These were six pretty little sea princesses; but the youngest was the most beautiful of all. Her skin was as clear and as fine as a rose leaf; her eyes were blue as the deepest sea; but, like all the rest, she had no feet, for her body ended in a fishtail.

Hans Christian Andersen

The Mermaid is a slip-cast porcelain doll. Her shoulder-plate head and lower limbs were formed in plaster molds. The porcelain pieces are attached to a fabric body. The doll's features and her shoes are china painted. Her hair is a light yellow mohair wig. She has two outfits. One is a mermaid suit featuring a green cotton tail that conceals her legs. The other costume is a short dress comprised of a pink dotted-swiss bodice and a blue skirt. Her undergarments include a white cotton half-slip and panties. She is 12 inches tall. The circumference of her head is 6½ inches.

15–2 The Mermaid.

The Head and Lower Limbs

To obtain a clear idea of the procedures that follow, read Chapter Thirteen, where detailed information regarding modeling, moldmaking, casting, and drying is presented. To make the porcelain doll parts you will need the following materials.

Materials

1½ pounds of modeling clay (oil- or water-base)
Mold boards
Approximately 6 pounds of potter's plaster
Porcelain slip (flesh-colored)
China paints

Make plastiline or water-clay models of the shoulder-plate head and lower limbs of the Mermaid. The photograph (fig. 15-5) can be used as a guide when modeling her features. Be sure the pieces are in proportion. Maintain simplicity to avoid undercuts. Model a lip and groove at the base of each limb (fig. 10-4). Model shoes on the legs of the doll (fig. 15-6). Slice off the back of the head (fig. 9-3). This doll does not have set-in eyes, but you may wish to use the mold for one that does. Attach collars and plugs (fig. 13-2).

If the models are constructed of water clay, allow the pieces to become leather-hard before proceeding.

Determine the dividing line on each piece. Bed the head in clay. Combine the lower limbs in one bed of clay (fig. 15-3).

Set the mold boards surrounding the beds. Mix plaster. Pour the first half of the molds.

When the plaster surface has cooled, remove the boards. Turn the models upside down. Remove the bed of clay. Clean the surface of the mold. Make keys. Reset the mold boards. Size both the plaster and the boards. Mix more plaster. Pour the second half of the molds. Give the plaster time to cool and harden.

Remove the boards. Open the molds. Take out the models. Close and band the molds. Set them aside to dry.

15–3   Limbs combined in one mold.

Clean the dry molds. Then pour each doll part, using flesh-colored porcelain slip.

Gently remove each set-up model. Fettle away mold seams and any other imperfections. Trim open the ends of the shoulder plate (fig. 15-4). Make holes in each lower corner of the shoulder plate (fig. 10-12).

At this point, if you prefer to attach the head to a ready-made composition body, cut off the shoulder plate where it joins the base of the neck. Moisten the cut edges of the clay. Smooth and shape the base of the neck so it will fit the neck socket of the purchased body.

Allow the pieces to become bone dry.

Fire the dry porcelain to cone 6 (2246° Fahrenheit). Cool.

Polish the surface of each piece satiny smooth. Wash and dry each doll part.

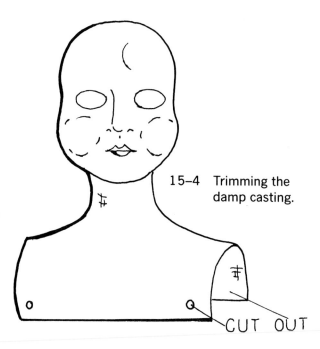

15–4   Trimming the damp casting.

CUT OUT

15-5 The Mermaid's
features.

China Painting

Use the photograph (fig. 15-5) as a guide and lightly sketch the features on the doll head. You can use a pencil. Any marks remaining will burn off when the china paint is fired. Also, lightly sketch the outline of the shoes (fig. 15-6) on the doll's feet.

Mix and paint the light colors first. Use red to color the cheeks, lips, nostrils, tear ducts, and ear lines. Remember, reds lose some of their brilliance when they are fired. Apply paint one shade darker than the final anticipated color. Paint the whites of the eyes and the white highlight in the center of the pupil. Fire the head to cone 018 (1328° Fahrenheit).

Mix brown china paint. Outline the lips and paint the eyebrows and tiny lashes rimming the lower edge of the eye. Use black china paint to color the shoes and the pupil of the eye, and outline the eye. Paint the iris of the eye blue. Fire the head and lower legs to cone 018 to set this final application of paint.

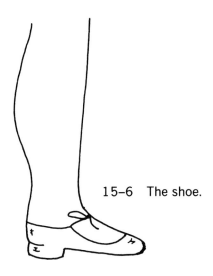

15-6 The shoe.

Assembling the Doll

Choose a sturdy flesh-colored fabric (such as Kettle Cloth) from which to cut the fabric body pieces. It should be strong without being bulky. It is difficult to turn small constructions right side out if they are made of heavy fabrics.

Materials

¼ yard of flesh-colored fabric from which to cut the
    body of the doll
White glue
Embroidery thread or sturdy twine for attaching
    porcelain to fabric
Thread to match the fabric
⅛ pound of polyester stuffing

Use the patterns as a guide (fig. 15-8) and cut two body pieces and four lower legs. Transfer all markings to the right side of the fabric.

Stitch together the shoulder seam of the two body pieces from the end of one arm to the end of the other (fig. 10-11). Turn ¼ inch of fabric along the base of each arm to the inside. Stitch close to the edge of these folded pieces, forming casing for drawstrings. Stitch the side seams and underarm seams. Do not stitch the casings closed. Leave an opening between one set of notches.

Stitch the base between the lower edges of the two body pieces (fig. 6-10). Turn the body right side out.

Assemble the upper legs. Begin by stitching together one side seam of one pair of leg pieces. Open out the piece. Turn ¼ inch of fabric to the inside along one narrow edge. Press and then stitch this edge in place, forming a casing for a drawstring (fig. 6-27). Stitch the second side seam, but do not stitch over the casing. Repeat this procedure and assemble the second leg.

Thread a drawstring through each casing. A 7-inch length of embroidery thread or sturdy string will do for each drawstring. Leave enough string dangling from each end of each casing to tie in a sturdy knot.

The porcelain limbs can now be attached to the fabric. To begin, coat the lip above the groove of one arm with white glue. Slip the arm inside the body through the side opening. Try to keep the glue from coming in contact with the fabric. Slip the porcelain hand out through the elbow opening of the arm. The base of the clay arm is wider than the fabric opening. The fabric should hold the piece, preventing it from slipping out of the body. Draw up the drawstring. It should slip into the groove in the porcelain arm. Tie the string in a sturdy knot. Add a touch of white glue to the knot to prevent its coming untied. Follow this procedure and attach the opposite arm. Attach the legs to the fabric upper legs.

Now, stuff the upper arms. Use tiny bits of stuffing. Avoid lumps. The arms should be full, yet soft. End stitching 1 inch below the stitching lines marked where the arms join the body. Stitch across these lines, twice. The stitching will create a joint and the arms will bend at the shoulder.

Stuff the body. It should be firmly stuffed. It must support the weight of the head. Turn ¼-inch fabric along the edges of the side opening to the inside.

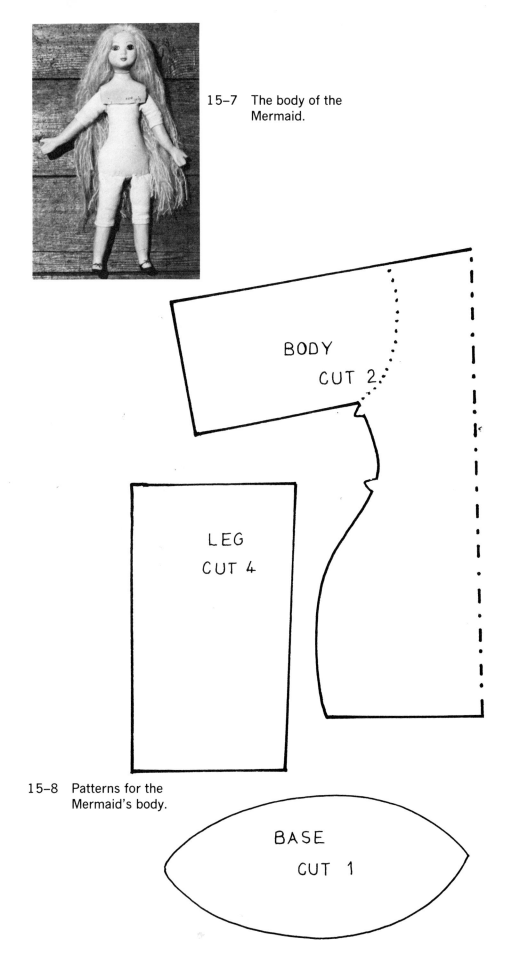

15-7 The body of the Mermaid.

BODY

CUT 2

LEG

CUT 4

15-8 Patterns for the Mermaid's body.

BASE

CUT 1

15–9 The Mermaid's
clothing.

Stitch these edges securely closed.

Stuff each upper leg. Like the arms, the legs should be full, yet soft. Turn ½ inch of fabric along the base of each leg to the inside. Stitch the opening closed. Securely stitch the base of each leg to the lower front of the body (fig. 6-15).

Now, the shoulder-plate head can be attached to the body. Hold the head and body in close proximity and loosely stitch an 8-inch length of embroidery thread or sturdy twine through the fabric of the body and out each hole in the shoulder plate (fig. 10-12). At each hole, leave an end of string dangling. Tip the head up, taking care not to pull the strings out of the fabric or plate. Coat the inside of the shoulder plate with white glue. Press the shoulder plate against the fabric. Draw up the strings and tie each in a sturdy knot. Place a drop of glue on the knots to hold them in place. Stretch a rubber band over the head and between the legs of the doll to hold the head tightly in position until the glue is dry. The Mermaid's body is assembled.

The Wig

The Mermaid's wig is constructed of pale yellow mohair yarn. Follow the instructions presented in Chapter Fourteen (subsection: "The Wig"), but observe the following change. Cut 15 yards of yarn into thirty 18-inch strands. It is not necessary for the Mermaid's wig to be as long as Rapunzel's. Make the wig. Attach it to the doll's head. Trim the finished wig and arrange the yarn so it sweeps back from her forehead.

The Clothing

The form of the Mermaid doll can be changed from a girl to a mermaid, simply by changing her clothes. The top of the mermaid suit is constructed of pale green knit fabric and decorated with bows of yellow embroidery thread. The tail is made of four layers of green cotton. The bodice of the dress is dotted swiss. The skirt is cotton. The sash is satin ribbon. The undergarments are white cotton. You can use these fabrics or substitute others; however, be sure to use a knit fabric for the top of the mermaid suit. It must stretch to fit. A list of materials necessary to make both costumes follows.

Materials

⅓ yard of green fabric (at least 40 inches wide) for
    the tail
A 10 x 12-inch scrap of knit fabric for the top
An 8 x 10-inch piece of fabric for the bodice of the
    dress
A 6 x 15-inch rectangle of fabric for the skirt
¼ yard of white cotton fabric for the undergarments
A 15-inch length of ¼-inch-wide elastic
A 16-inch length of ¼-inch-wide satin ribbon
Embroidery thread
3 tiny snap closures
Thread to match the fabrics
A handful of polyester stuffing

Use the patterns (figs. 15-10, 15-11, 15-12) and cut the number of pieces necessary for the Mermaid's two outfits. Also, cut a rectangle measuring 6 x 15 inches for the skirt of the dress. Cut a rectangle measuring 6 x 12 inches for the slip. Transfer all markings to the wrong side of the fabric.

THE MERMAID SUIT. Stitch the perimeter of one pair of tail pieces together, leaving the notched edges unstitched (fig. 15-13). Stitch together the second pair. Turn both right side out and press. Place a slender pad of stuffing in the base of each tail.

Stitch the notched lower edge of each bodice piece to the notched edge of one tail piece (right sides together). Cut a 2-inch slit from the neck edge, down the center of one bodice piece. This will be the back of the outfit. Hem the edges of the slit. Stitch the two bodice pieces together, along the shoulder seams. Stitch the underarm seams of the bodice to the point where they join the tail. Turn the bodice right side out.

Top-stitch the tail sections together. Place the line of stitching ¼ inch within the edge and use a contrasting color of thread. Stitch around the perimeter, beginning and ending stitching at the waist edge of the bodice.

Hem the neck edge and the ends of the sleeves. Stitch a bow of brightly colored embroidery thread to the center front of the neck, the sleeves, and the waist. Stitch a snap closure to the neck edge of the slit. Press.

THE PANTIES. Stitch together one side seam of the pair of pantie pieces. Open out the piece. Turn and press ½ inch of fabric along the waist edge to the inside. Stitch close to the edge of the pressed piece, forming a casing for elastic (fig. 6-21). Thread a 5-inch length of ¼ inch-wide elastic through the casing. Stitch the elastic securely to both ends of the casing. Stitch the second side seam. Stitch the crotch seam. Hem the base of the legs. Press.

THE SLIP. Following the above procedure, make a casing for elastic along one long edge of the rectangle of slip fabric (fig. 6-21). Thread a 5-inch length of elastic through the casing. Stitch it securely to both ends. Stitch the narrow ends of the rectangle of fabric together from the waist edge to the base of the slip. Hem the lower edge. Press.

THE DRESS. The front of the dress bodice is decorated with four tucks stitched permanently in place. Note the stitching lines marked on the bodice fabric. Refer to figure 15-14. Draw together one pair of dotted lines. The fabric should be pressed together with the lines overlapping one another. Stitch over the dotted lines. Repeat, stitching the three remaining tucks.

Stitch the shoulder seams of the bodice front to the bodice back (fig. 7-14). Hem the neck edge and the back opening edges. Then, turn ½ inch of fabric

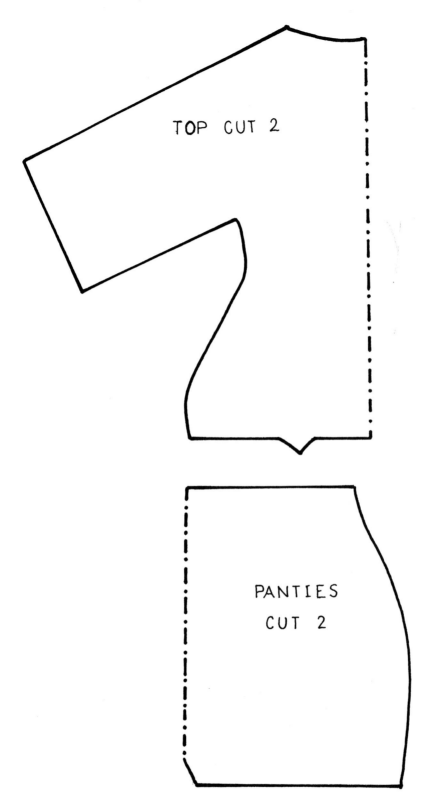

TOP CUT 2

PANTIES
CUT 2

15–10   Patterns for the Mermaid's clothing.

172   *THE MERMAID*

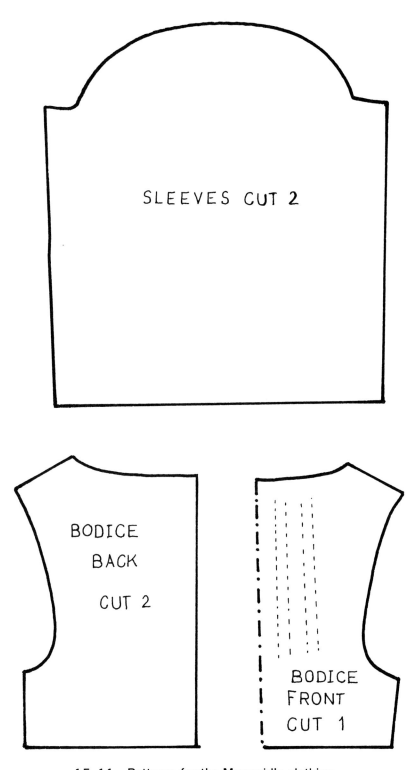

SLEEVES CUT 2

BODICE
BACK

CUT 2

BODICE
FRONT
CUT 1

15-11   Patterns for the Mermaid's clothing.

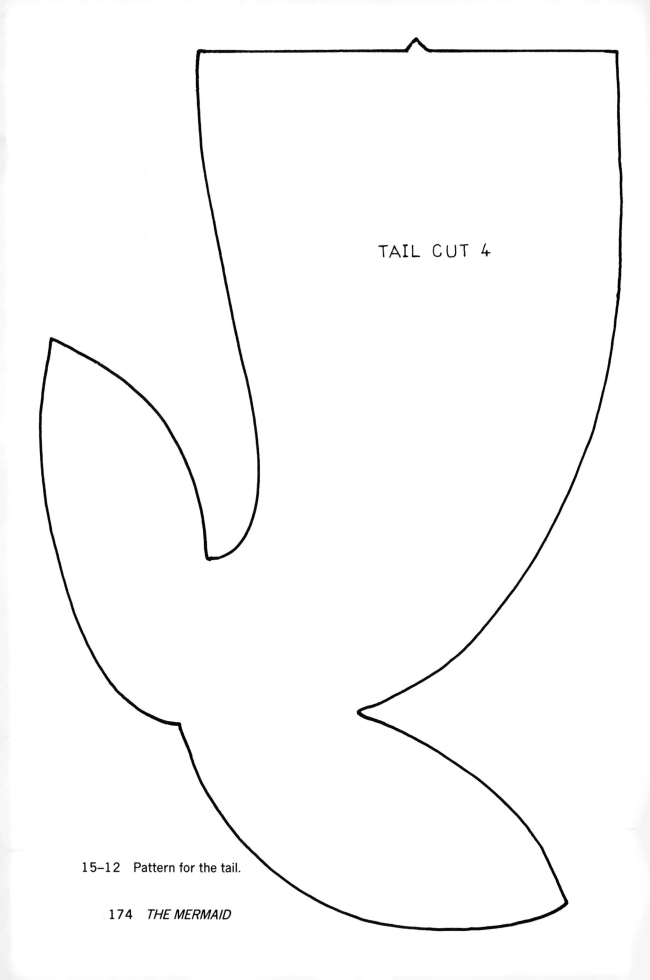

TAIL CUT 4

15–12   Pattern for the tail.

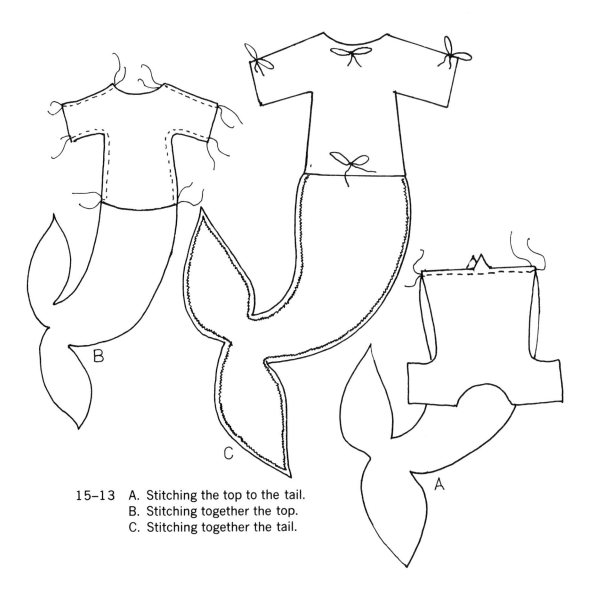

15–13 A. Stitching the top to the tail.
       B. Stitching together the top.
       C. Stitching together the tail.

along the wrist end of each sleeve to the inside. Press and then stitch close to the edge of each folded piece, forming a casing for elastic (fig. 6-21). Thread a 2½-inch length of elastic through each casing. Stitch the elastic to the ends of the casing. Next, run a line of basting stitches ⅛ inch within the curved end of each sleeve. Draw up stitching, slightly gathering the sleeve. Align and baste (adjusting the gathers) a sleeve to each armhole. Stitch the sleeves to the bodice. Stitch the underarm seams.

To attach the skirt, run a line of basting stitches ⅛ inch within one long edge of the rectangle of skirt fabric. Draw up the stitching, gathering the edge to the length of the waist edge of the bodice. With right sides together, pin, baste, and stitch the gathered edge of the skirt to the waist edge of the bodice (fig. 8-15).

Stitch the back of the skirt together from the base to within 1 inch of the waist of the bodice. Hem the raw edges of the opening. Hem the lower edge of the skirt. Stitch a tiny snap closure to the neck and waist of the back-opening edges of the bodice. Press. When the dress is on the Mermaid, tack the length of satin ribbon around the waist for a sash. Project Eight, the Mermaid, is complete.

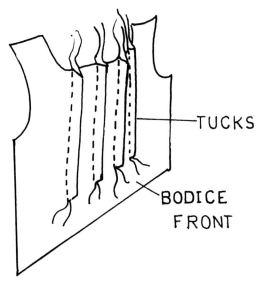

TUCKS

BODICE
FRONT

15-14 Stitching tucks on the
bodice front.

In conclusion, I hope the preceding pages will serve as a point of departure, guiding craftspeople/artists toward the production of beautiful, original dolls of composition, bisque, and porcelain.

GLOSSARY OF TERMS

Air Bubbles Pockets of air in a liquid that will create pinholes in the surface of a mold or casting.

Air Pockets Small hollows containing air, which can be present within the walls of clay constructions.

Armature An internal support for plastic modeling compounds.

Atmospheric Water Water present, in varying degrees, in bone-dry clay. A result of humidity.

Bats Forms made of plaster and used when wedging, modeling, and drying clay.

Bedding Encasing a portion of a model in clay, creating a dividing line for the mold.

Bisque Ceramic clay that has been fired only once. Also defined by doll-makers as unglazed porcelain.

Bone Dry Clay that no longer contains water of plasticity.

Casing A tunnel of fabric through which elastic or drawstrings are threaded.

China Glazed porcelain.

Chemically Combined Water Water that is part of the molecular structure of clay.

Circumference The distance around the perimeter of a circle.

Clay Body A blend of two or more clays plus other additives.

Composition A modeling compound composed of paper, glue, and other materials that is plastic when wet, but dries hard and durable.

Deflocculation A process that turns plastic clay into liquid by destroying the attraction of clay particles for one another.

Diameter The distance across a circle.

Draft The point of division and the direction of movement of a mold away from a cast piece.

Fettling Trimming clay from a damp, unfired ceramic piece.

Firing Cycle   The period that clay spends subjected to high temperatures inside a kiln while maturing.

Flux   A substance added to a clay body to bond the materials together, causing them to mature at a lower temperature than would otherwise be natural.

Greenware   Unfired, but hard, clay pieces.

Hydrated Alumina   A dry, powdered ingredient clay used as an alternative to a kiln wash when firing procelain doll parts.

Inside of Fabric   The side of the fabric that will not be seen when the garment is finished.

Kaolin   A refractory residual clay, the main ingredient of porcelain.

Keys   Notches carved into the surface of the mold to help assure that the pieces will close tightly and accurately.

Kiln   A piece of equipment, like an oven, that reaches high temperatures to fire ceramic clays.

Kraft Paper   A strong, unbleached brown paper often used for bags.

Leather-hard   Clay that is no longer plastic but can still be carved.

Linseed Oil   A drying oil used in making composition.

Liquid Latex   Liquid rubber casting compound that also makes an excellent adhesive for bonding fabrics.

Matured   Clay which has reached maximum hardness during firing.

Model   To shape a plastic medium, or the sculptured object itself.

Mold   A plaster form used to hold slip or composition in a shape until it hardens.

Oil Clay   Clay particles suspended in oil. This clay does not harden.

Outside of Fabric   The side of the fabric that will be visible when the garment is completed.

Perimeter   The outside edge of a shape or form.

Plastic   A compound that can be modeled.

Plasticizer   A solution that will turn clay slip into modeling clay by causing the particles to regain their attraction for one another.

Plastiline   An oil-base clay.

Plug   A clay shape attached to the base of a prototype to provide a channel for the entry of slip or air into a plaster mold.

Porcelain   A clay body that fires white and translucent at high temperatures.

Potter's Plaster   A grade of plaster especially formulated for moldmaking.

Prototype   The model of a doll from which a mold is made.

Pyrometer   A device that indicates the exact temperature inside a kiln.

Pyrometric cone   A small clay pyramid that bends at specific temperatures indicating kiln temperature.

Residual   Clay that has remained where it was formed.

Retaining Walls   Mold boards or other materials employed to hold liquid plaster in place until it hardens.

Sedimentary   Clay that has moved from its place of origin.

Set-up   A process of crystallization during which plaster turns from a liquid to a solid. Clay slip also sets up.

Shim   A metal or plastic piece pressed into the clay of a model and used to hold back liquid plaster, creating dividing points for the pieces of the mold.

Shoulder-plate head   A doll head with an extension from the base of the neck that is used to attach the head to a fabric body.

Size   A coating applied to a surface to prevent plaster from adhering to it.

Slaking   Period during which plaster is not stirred while it absorbs water.

Slip   Liquid water-base clay that has been deflocculated.

Slurry   Water-thinned clay that has not been deflocculated.

Swivel Head   A doll head attached to a body in such a manner that it can turn within the neck socket.

Talc   A flux that causes clay to harden at low temperatures.

Template   A pattern or guide, usually geometric shapes cut out of thin plastic.

Undercut   An area within a mold that is wider than the mold opening.

Vitrification   The point during the firing cycle at which porcelain glassifies.

Water Clay   Clay that is plastic because it contains water. This clay hardens but must be fired to mature.

Water of Plasticity   Water which, in combination with clay particles, makes clay plastic.

Water Smoking Period   The segment of the firing cycle during which atmospheric water evaporates.

Wedging   Kneading, dividing, and recombining clay to eliminate air pockets and develop an even consistency.

White Glue   An excellent adhesive for bonding porous materials. Elmer's glue is an example of white glue.

Whiting   Pure white chalk or calcium carbonate used in composition and gesso.

BOOKS AND PUBLICATIONS OF INTEREST TO __THE DOLLMAKER__

BOOKS

Boehn, Max von. *Dolls*. New York: Dover, 1972.

Coleman, Dorothy S., Elizabeth A., and Evelyn J. *The Collector's Encyclopedia of Dolls*. New York: Crown Publishers, Inc., 1968.

Farris, Edmond J. *Art Students' Anatomy*. New York: Dover Press, 1953.

Kenny, John B. *Ceramic Sculpture*. Radnor, Pennsylvania: Chilton Book Co., 1953.

Nicolaides, Kimon. *The Natural Way to Draw*. Boston: Houghton Mifflin Company, 1941.

Rothenberg, Polly. *The Complete Book of Ceramic Art*. New York: Crown Publishers, Inc., 1972.

Seeley, Mildred D. *Porcelain and Low-Fire Doll Making*. Oneonta, New York: Seeley's Ceramic Service, Inc., 1973.

Seeley, Mildred and Vernon. Making Original Dolls and Molds. Oneonta, New York: Seeley's Ceramic Service, Inc., 1977.

Taubes, Frederic. *Acrylic Painting for the Beginner*. New York: Watson-Guptill, 1971.

Taylor, Doris W., and Hart, Anne Button. *China Painting*. New York: Van Nostrand Reinhold Company, 1962.

PUBLICATIONS

The Doll Artisan. Seeley's Ceramic Service, Inc., 9 River Street, Oneonta, New York 13820 (published bimonthly).

The Dollmaker. Castle Press Publications Inc. P.O. Box 247, Washington, New Jersey 07882 (published bimonthly).

SOURCES OF SUPPLY

Bell Yarn Company
75 Essex Street
New York, N.Y. 10002

Mail Order: 35 Clay St.
             Brooklyn, N.Y. 11222

Mohair yarn

Flax Artists' Materials
57 West Grand Avenue
Chicago, Ill. 60601

Also stores in Los Angeles
               New York
               San Francisco

Acrylic gesso, paints, varnish
Armature wire
Brushes
Liquid latex
Modeling tools
Pens and points
Roma Plastilina
Whiting
X-Acto knives
Other painting and modeling
    supplies

Dollpart Supply Company, Inc.
5-06 51st Avenue
Long Island City, N.Y. 11101

Blown-glass eyes
Doll wigs
Eyelashes
Skull crowns (buckram)
Wooden neck buttons
Other dollmaking accessories

Doll Repair Parts Inc.
9918 Lorain Avenue
Cleveland, Ohio 44102

Blown-glass eyes
Composition bodies
Wigs
Wooden neck buttons
Other dollmaking accessories

Miller Ceramics
Weedsport, N.Y. 13166

Hydrated alumina
Kilns
Modeling tools
Nichrome wire
Porcelain modeling clay
Pyrometric cones
Sodium silicate
White talc modeling clay
Whiting
Other supplies for ceramicists

New York Central Supply
62 Third Avenue
New York, N.Y. 10003

Acrylic gesso, paints, varnish
Armature wire
Brushes
Liquid latex
Modeling tools
Pens and points

Roma Plastilina
Templates
Whiting
X-Acto knives
Other supplies for artists

Putnam Company, Inc.   Polyester stuffing
Box 310
Walworth, WI. 53184

Schoepfer Eyes   Blown-glass eyes
138 West 31st Street
New York, N.Y. 10001

Sculpture House   Kilns
38 East 30th St.   Liquid latex
New York, N.Y. 10016   Modeling tools
                                        Mold soap
                                        Potter's plaster
                                        Pyrometric cones
                                        Roma Plastilina
                                        Sculpta Mold
                                        Shellac
                                        S. H. Royal porcelain
                                        White talc modeling clay
                                        Wire
                                        Other supplies for sculptors

Seeley's Ceramic Service, Inc.   Bisque stains and sealer
9 River Street   Brushes
Oneonta, N.Y. 13820   China paints and mediums
                                        Coloring agents for slip
                                        Composition bodies
                                        Eye molds
                                        Hydrated alumina
                                        Kiln elements
                                        Kilns and Test kilns
                                        Modeling tools
                                        Mold bands
                                        Mold soap
                                        Nichrome wire
                                        Pens and points
                                        Plasticizer
                                        Porcelain slip (white and flesh-
                                        colored)
                                        Potter's plaster
                                        Rubber neck stoppers
                                        Sculpta Mold
                                        White talc clay
                                        Other dollmaking and ceramic
                                        supplies

Standard Doll Company   Glass eyes
23-83 31st Street   Dolls wigs
Long Island City, N.Y. 11105   Other dollmaking accessories

INDEX